~ Random ~

Random

#180

~ the choices we have forgotten about ~

Cover photo credits:
Photographer: *Peter Mercieca*
Model: *Nicole Ebejer*
Design: *Kevin Busuttil* at *alignedheart.com*

~ Random ~

Dedication:

My Father, Mother, Brother…who with me, withstood all the hardships, and dusty taste of despair…and who with me, have risen. To them, I owe my LIFE.

My Grandmother…who's fragile yet immortal presence, reigns over my Heart supreme.

To my "Friends" …who's number don't exceed the fingers of both hands.

~

This time I thought of mentioning some names of people, that have inspired me, maybe without even knowing, through their own unique self-expression;
Kevin (B), Christine (H), Simon Paul (S), William (B), Akash (S), Christina (P), Andra (C), Nicole (E), Denise (G), and Kira (D).
Thanks to Peter Mercieca (photography) for sticking out my perfectionism through the photo-shoot, and for managing to portray my vision in form; thank you!

To you…
Who have tasted the bitterness of pain.
Who came forth into Light, from within the dark.

Last, and the most important, is the One that carries no name; Life.

We are, what we seek.

∞

~ Random ~

What is Random?

Random is a series of events, and alternate realties within my perception, that went on during these last three years. These "realities", differ from one another as if it is not the same person that is experiencing them. Yet, the one who sees and writes, has never changed. In the storm of experience, I would be the one merging interchangeably with Life's sensual dance of creation. An energy that penetrates me like the breath that goes through the lungs, to finally show in the sharing of the Pen's tip with Paper.

Sometimes it is hurried, for while I am engulfed in "its" womb, my mouth and hands have to move themselves to words; for a visual and literal description of all that is going on. An experience shall never be repeated twice, hence why I write; out of my own attachment to Life. So you will find spellings and grammatical mistakes throughout the texts, for I was only the one that had to record them fast so they won't get lost to the passing of time. I could have done proof-reading, but I didn't, because I wanted the reader to feel, and get into what I felt; that ecstatic frenzy and yet calmness, similar to that of love-making. These mistakes may, or may not, be judged by the reader's mind, yet, there will be a stronger flow, that of words in rhythm, which have the power to move you forward and around. If you get stuck in judgment, it is of *your own choice*. Observing all this, will show the attitude one adopts throughout Life. In here, am just describing my journey as a human on Earth, with words. Simply "lost" in this wondrous world.

Random is desire, lust, and the attachment to an illusion.
Random is dreams, intimacy, and the longing for love.
Random is a pause within eternity.
Random is Human.

~

~ Random ~

Introduction:

It all started in 2009 while in a full-blown heroin addiction. The trigger? A Nietzsche pocket book, and a girl.

In between injecting myself, pondering about life, and all of a sudden dating this girl...words started coming. The beauty of her skin, the light transmitted by her hair, and the daily ecstatic orgasms, were the lines between which my pen flowed.

As all else, nothing lasts. My obsessive and compulsive frame of mind, was making the air unbreathable within our relationship. She had to leave...and I was once again left alone with needles and tears. Now, nothing obstructed my path of self-destruction. For the remaining four years, my drug habit increased, until it finally landed me in jail for stealing precious jewellery from my parents. Amongst that jewellery, was the only legacy my father, and our family, had of his mother. The most beloved woman in our lives.

While in jail for a couple of months, living in very confined spaces, I started observing the behaviour of others, making me learn more about my own. I asked my family to bring me some books, a diary, and my small collection of Parker Pens. In there, within high walls and barred windows, I have built my own free world, where the line of communication between me and GOD, were a pen and a paper.

Next in line, were four months of Rehab in an institution that works with the principles of The Twelve Steps, founded on the basis that addiction is a Spiritual disease. It is here, that I found what I was always searching for. In those walls, I had wet dreams at night and visions in day light. One afternoon, while having lunch, all of a sudden, Past and Future came into one soft swift transition.

~ Random ~

They showed themselves to me, with the seductive allure of the Female embodiment. Hurriedly, I finished my lunch, and went straight to my notebook to wed all to paper. There came to Life the poem; *The Death of Night*.

In here, all bodies have become one. Once separate, they are now a breathable body, of song, dance, tears, and love. So, forget for a moment who you are, the problems, worries and fear that come with that. Just be the one that swims through the absence of words within these pages. Be the Life, out and beyond fear. You are here, and wherever, by "own" choice.

~

"These words came to me like the stars that adorn the night.
Yet, don't seek me among them, for they are only a magic spell, that
Life has casted upon me.

Leave your understanding at the cover of this book,
and let your own yearning for Love, guide you through it.

See yourself beyond all imagination.
Let the words lose their meaning."

~

Let Love not escape you

Thank You

~ Random ~

Who is SHE?

Sometimes, I think that no woman can fill this space that SHE occupies within me. Don't get me wrong, I love women, and everything about them; such fierce earthly creatures. If Man is able to drive countries to war, and to the edge of insanity, Woman can take you to the rugged edges of space, and leave you there, marinating within a womb that pledges creation. My gaze, is all theirs', for every sounding move they make, sings about that still in time, where they undress from the decadent gown which is mankind. SHE, is an ideal, a fabrication of my own desires, that moves around my bed at night, weaving for me sheets of dreams. Upon this bed, I am dead, for it is the alchemy of Souls, to turn stone into gold.

SHE comes to me with the infinite facets, of the Women that inhabit this space. They are the droplets that make up Her ocean, of waves and voluptuous curves.

SHE is the Woman in me.
The Utopian Androgyny.
It is Life, in its complex simplicity.

S pace
H eart
E xistence

* where the word "you" is mentioned, I am at times referring to myself. While in other instances, "you" is in reference to a specific person within a dialogue.
* where the word "She" or "Her" are mentioned, most times there is no particular woman, but I am relating to an ideal, or to the energy of Life itself. Other times there is a particular woman in play.

How you will perceive it, is totally up to you.

~ Random ~

*"To find your Soulmate,
First you have to find your Soul.*

*When that is done,
You will see that;
There is nothing else
To find."*

~ Random ~

The Death of Night

In the dark of night…in the glimmer of day…She came!
Under the most shadowy of cloaks…the most radiant of
cloaks…concealing the dagger in her hand, to slay the Life in me.

She pierced my heart…kissed my eyes…blew on my lips.
Enchanted I so was; by her fierce blood-shot eyes…by her
transparent icy skin…by her ruby glittering scarlet hair – for so
intense it was, representing all of mankind sins.
Under her spell, I fell…rotten was my heart…abandoned all hope
my eyes… and only villainy spoke my lips.

Farther away I searched…for someone who could save me from
this seductress…from this infatuation…to whom shackled I was
with the heaviest of chains, and the most damned of armours.

Than…barefooted…under no disguise…SHE came!
The Goddess that reigns my dreams.
With all her simplicity…dressed with only the lightest of ivory
cloths…nothing SHE left to the imagination of man.
For SHE had no sin…no shame.

Her unconditional love…her passion for Life…melted away the
cold steel that dressed my skin…gave me feathered wings…freed
my soul - in deliverance to the Whole!

You…me…me in you…you around me…BLEED! BLEED!
BLEED the warm waters of Life-
Deliver us to one!

05.12.2013 (in Drug Rehabilitation, Gozo)

~ Random ~

Alexandria

Skin soft and pale as a thread of silk,
Hair black as a raven's feather.
Almond shaped eyes…dark and deep, as the night sky with its moon and all its stars.
All, adorned with a smile, that glows fierce fully as the morning Sun.

04.11.2013 (in Drug Rehabilitation, Gozo)

~ Random ~

Autumn Leaves

An Autumn gathering of trees,
Shedding their leaves...
Red and brown foliage cover the ground...
- Sharp gentle features, you're to age not bound.
Ivory mist blankets this soil, sacred...
- The fragrance of your skin, naked.
On each leaf your name written,
On each tree your face a vision.
Under all of them Life hides,
Dark brown as your ever-speaking,
ever-smouldering eyes.
In surrender I bow to thee,
For I found You in Me.

16.03.2014 (a dream. Her is Nature, the ultimate Lover)

~ Random ~

Butterfly Girl

She sits quietly staring at the pages full of words in front of her.
Tattooed butterflies scattered on her back,
as if she's a flower herself.
The warm sea breeze carries the fragrance of her salty skin.
The sun hides behind, defining her body of joyful splendour,
While burning away doubts...
GOD is perfection,
Making the Woman a pure symbol of creation.

14.07.2014 (perceived from a stranger, St. Paul's Bay, Malta)

~ Random ~

Existence

As the Sun embraces the infinite Sea...
As the Moon kisses the reddening Sky...
As the Stars look to each other and smile...

In silence rules Lord Shiva's beat,
Relentless waves embrace her feet.
Destined footsteps on soft wet sand,
Writing fading words with her hand.
Gentle wind blows Life through her hair,
She is Existence, laying herself bare.

15.07.2014 (a vision)

~ Random ~

Twenty Fingers

I lay next to you at night,
looking at that God given face.
In bed our bodies - space!

Listening to the stream of breaths,
Feel the beat coming from your chest
The natural movement of your breast.

Our hands entangled, above:
Twenty fingers making Love.

09.12.2014 (a desire)

~ Random ~

Teal Sheets

In the midst of a crowd,
surrounded with loud voices 'n' noises,
You take in yours, my shaking hand.
We made our way, far faraway,
Resting down on pillows of hay.

Under teal coloured sheets,
In open mind fields...
Clouds upon us gaze,
Butterflies each other chase.

There is pleasure and desire in knowing.
But the greatest action I can ever do,
Is to love what I will never know about you.

09.01.2015 (after a sexual intimate moment, Mellieha)

~ Random ~

Wave

Let me dance on top of you.
Let me sing your name.
Let me get lost in your hair.
Let me play hide and seek in your bed.
Let me count you countless times.
Let me shower with your salty tears.
Let me fly underneath your skin.
Let me rest on your shores.
Let me play in your embrace.
- Oh, fierce gentle wave.

12.01.2015 (watching the sea, Kalkara)

~ Random ~

Fox

I stay arm's length away,
To see all of you,
To long your touch,
And have you by desire.
I sleep next to your feet,
Just to imagine what it will be like.
I put my head to rest,
At the end of your hair,
Just to have something of you on my face.
I bundle up as a fox and its tail,
Protecting with ferocity his wintry sleep,
Surrounded with silence and its savagery.

17.01.2015 (extract from my first ceremony)

~ Random ~

Nirvana

Immersion of star-like eyes,
A desire they ignite;
to growl and howl,
to bite and scratch,
at this flesh.

Her lamented cry - a vehement call,
resonates through the ribs of my chest,
Taking me to a primordial land,
where the bloody death of illusion,
marks the path.

There, She welcomes me in all nakedness...
Breathing unto me her tropical winds,
As my lust melts away, like wax near fire.
Like a repentant child, I am on my knees,
She holds my face gently to her belly,
And with my hands circling around her woven legs,
We dive deep into streams of molten earth.

Moon takes his leave behind the dark of night.
Falling from the sky...stars and tears alike...
Greet my arrival to Nirvana.

18.12.2015 (extract from my first ceremony)

~ Random ~

Her wake up

Wind blows at the sleeping sea,
In his desire to kiss and dance.
Volcanic fires tell an ancient tale.
Humid forests whisper Aztec songs.
Snowy mountains play a thundering drum.
Silent arid deserts roar an ode of desolation.
Gazelles thump, their hooves to the beat.
Lions sink, their claws in a killing dance.
Eagles feed their young, in feathers stained with blood.
Rabbits in holes, laughing toothily after cheating a fleeting death.
Flowers in vanity, hang their skirts to spread flamboyance.

Courted by the sweet melancholic moon,
as he grows impatient in his wait...
Still sleepy under her blanket of stars,
from her eyes, tears, as comets in the sky.
All creation is in fervent celebration,
for Her 3000 year old slumber is at its end.
She! Is waking up...

18.12.2015 (extract from my first ceremony)

~ Random ~

I am for all Time

Bedroom window...
masked with dew...
from last night breaths.
In my garden...
with just a shirt...
cigarette in hand...
smoke not wanting to leave your lips...
mist flows round your naked hips.
In reverence...
collecting berries,
to wash away an undesired taste.
I hide behind curtains,
gazing at you,
dancing in the depths of soul.
Flowers look up, and blush,
at your skin's touch.
Skinny branches,
like fingers on a piano,
let go of their autumn leaves.
You start seeking,
questioning if I left.
You find my writing on the window pane,
saying that I am... there... here
- whispering softly,
a song of longing.
I am for all time...
that ghostly presence you felt since child,
to whom you just made love.

27.01.2015 (written in rainy weather, looking out from behind a window in desire)

~ Random ~

The Edge of Now

Wake up from under those prison sheets,
that comfortable bed is sinking.
I feel thunder rolling through your soul,
Come...come, don't hide anymore.
Let's run...run to dark and unknown places,
We will twist...mould faiths and faces.
Hand in hand we'll run...run forever...run,
Let's not wait for our turn to die.
Come...come...run on the edge with me now.

19.02.2015 (...)

~ Random ~

Let me in!

Deep in my sleep,
I heard an old man's weep.
He was the Moon, asking me to fly,
To go to him as thunder through the sky.
- High!
I arrived there with my heart full of pains,
Finding you imprisoned in your own chains.
Looking into each other's eyes,
We filled the air with our cries.
"Let me in!" - I asked.
"I am afraid." - you replied.
So, I imprisoned my Self in your body,
Metal links turning to blood with our folly.
With the Moon as our cradle,
We burned as fire,
In our loving desire.

05.03.2015 (a dream)

~ Random ~

Virgin White

Strange things happened this night,
Where the Sun was out of sight.
The Past a fearful ghost,
The Future a long-lost host.
The baffling time was in doom,
Stopped was the pendulum.

A rebellious revolution,
A backward evolution.
My Soul to you flew,
Over Seas of blue.
Together we went in virgin white,
To the marriage of darkness and light.

03.03.2015 (a dream)

~ Random ~

*We are in a dreaming state,
where the dream itself is trying to wake us up.*

~ Random ~

Deity

When I look into your eyes,
I see clouds revolving in the skies.
A 1000 births of butterflies.
A hurricane of stars.
Melting away prison bars.
A fountain of flowers.
A deity with divine powers.

05.03.2015 (my vision of Life's transcendence from a specific woman)

~ Random ~

Behind Drama

Behind a veil of theatrical melodies,
In my weak arms, she cries,
I kiss and drink from her wet eyes.
Over a drunken daze, we sold our lucidity,
In a tear, the fear of vulnerability.

A wandering lonely Soul...
Dances to the sound of a singing bowl.

What calls Who?

Is it You?

23.03.2015 (after a consoling moment with my girlfriend at the time, Kalkara)

~ Random ~

The Land of Eerie

Do you know of the feeling when entering a cave, while outside, the cold wind blows so hard that it feels like it is tearing off your skin - a devilish rupture?

The first assimilation of my senses; the welcoming warm humid air, the cosines that reminds me of home - the womb... where all exterior sounds and noises fade, in the echoing melody of water droplets, falling gracefully to their destiny of rock. I placed myself in the depths of the cave. Staring at walls, that recited the story written in scars on my own body;

"My my, let us sing this poor boy a lullaby - bye!
Let his sickening anguish,
Through our water perish!
Drink the sour tea,
From the sacred tree.
Chew the hardened root,
In it you'll find wisdom
- and truth.
With Her kiss, a drunken taste of mint,
She will take you through the labyrinth.
Now! ...the puzzled query...
Are you ready for the land of eerie?"
- said the Walls.

26.03.2015 (a dream, in reference to the brew)

~ Random ~

Head on Pillow

I put my head on the pillow, and feel the total unrest of my body. The fragrance you left behind, tells me that you're not here.

Where shall I search for you?

I drown myself in sheets for the vain attempt of find a position where I can feel your embrace. The earthly smell of fire and soil of your hair, drifts me off to a drowsy sleep.

To my elation, I see a vision of you waiting for me on the other side of a bridge, with a protruding hand in longing. Inebriated, with the taste of each other's sweat, in dream this night we celebrate.

30.03.2015 (between reality and dream, not wanting to surrender at her departure)

~ Random ~

The Birth of Dawn

Thousand and one deaths,
tasting of mermaids' breath.

Nine and nine spitting knives,
waking the nightmares at night.

Behind the six-faced mask, a flaming eye,
burning angels' wings right off the sky.

Between her legs my licking tongue,
praising the lives of the yet unsung.

All hail the bloody birth of dawn,
She is our only way Home.

09.04.2015 (...)

~ Random ~

She comes without a Name

Let me tell you about Her...
She looks at me from a pair of eyes drawn on butterfly's wings...
deep and kind.

She talks to me from within a flower bud... untainted and innocent.

She touches me as Sea does to the sandy Shore... pushing and
pulling me relentlessly towards Her.

She just knows how much to give and take... for me to have All,
yet not enough.

Her name is Life.

24.04.2015 (...)

~ Random ~

Romeo & Juliette

Oh Juliette, you gave yourself away in the name of love.
Oh Romeo, you that for your beloved tainted yourself with blood.

>In front of God you swore,
>through peace and war,
>Against families and kin,
>Sacrificing your own skin,
>To be together,
>- In nowhere.

05.05.2015(…)

~ Random ~

The Goddess Kali

Fearsome grieving Lady...
Maiden of Fire...
Body of burning ashes...

Lay waste to man's thoughts,
Destroy all illusion and hope.

Ruler of anarchic fate,
Together, tonight...
In blood, we bathe.

08.05.2015 (from my connection with the energy of destruction)

~ Random ~

My Blood & Bone

Tears of a widow,
in procession follow.
Children in streets play,
with only a laugh to say.
Old people with birds in hand,
telling tales of ancient land.
Soldiers each other kill,
for others to make there fill.

We denied ourselves for far too long,
Oh my blood and bone!
Kings, and Queens without a throne.
Oh this poem and song,
Written with my blood and bone!

Clouds fade in the sky away,
no one is destined here to stay.
Cars confusingly passing by,
Seeds in search of soil they fly.
Hanging to the lips of my Lover,
I honestly seek no other.
Breaths taking time,
Words no longer rhyme.

cont...

~ Random ~

My Blood & Bone
cont…

I am just a faceless wanderer,
A secret bearer,
With just his story to share,
And forever roam in here.
Patiently I'll fade,
Gently in the shade...

It's time to say no more!
To those that made us whore.
Same skin all kin,
Oh my blood and bone,
Turn your lights on!
Let us rise to this new dawn,
Oh my blood and bone!

14.05.2015 (…)

~ Random ~

Come Together

We are stars that die,
For infinity, multiply.
A sweet-sour wine,
Essence of love divine.
An eternal flame,
Erasing our shame.

Vow to be generous and kind,
Before we leave all this behind.
Open are my wondering eyes,
Seeing above the translucent sky.
Let's come, and come together,
Roaming in this space of forever.

16.05.2016 (…)

~ Random ~

Silky Spider Web

Silky spider web threads, is her hair.
The setting sun makes of her skin a flare.
Father Moon in her presence blushes,
In thirsty soil, she buries her grudges.
She roams in open fields,
While her air I breathe.

02.06.2015 (while looking at my girl-friend at the time)

~ Random ~

A Forsaken God

Empty darken faces,
Roaming desolate places.

Kings on thrones aflame,
Pointing fingers by blame,
Drowning their nature in shame.

Let it sleep that hungry beast,
On its flesh in fire we'll feast.

Man, coming out of the female cunt,
Desperately going through the night in hunt.

A forsaken god garrisoned in stone temples,
For the misery of man to bread and wine, put in shackles.

Her drunken eyes offer all humanity freedom,
We, that were born without sin and full of wisdom.

Leave behind your deeds,
For it is your ego, they feed.

06.06.2015 (current state of world affairs)

~ Random ~

Hidden Truth

We've been fed a promise in vain,
Which drive us all insane.

They've hid from us the truth,
Separating the tree from its root.

Cutting off our wings so not to fly,
Making us fear what lies in the sky.

Hold your hands together,
To rule from now and forever.

God, is you,
All that is new.

09.06.2015 (…)

~ Random ~

Million Smokes

From the horizon, She rises,
As birds whisper praises,

Mermaids knit her a dress in lace,
Sunlight covers her body and face.

With a tongue in million smokes,
The death of illusion She evokes.

Burning those that in greediness roam,
Drowning fears in thundering storms.

Her roaring breath for our souls a call,
In surrender and acceptance, I fall.

15.06.2015 (inspired by the "divine" feminine)

~ Random ~

Haze

I've been holding on to vain promises,
Finding rest in false hopes and kisses.

Just wanted to rest my weary head on clouds,
When death came, and took away my spouse.

Scratched bluntly the flesh on my body,
In search for all that is sacred and holy.

Fingers stained with blood,
Knees bent touching the ground.

Air, whispering words to itself,
Heart in flames and burning flesh.

Skies - ablaze,
Life - a haze.

19.06.2015 (from my relation with Life)

~ Random ~

Life is transparent, yet not invisible.
Life is illusive, yet real.

~ Random ~

Mistress of the Unknown

Shaking, I got up from my chair,
Heart beating faster and faster.

She told me -
"You will never know,
The magic of flow,
Until you let go!"

So, I took Her by the hand,
With that rose in her hair and said -
"Ok, let's dance alone,
Mistress of the unknown!"

30.06.2016 (what I experienced, that pushed me to give my resignation from an office job)

~ Random ~

No Labels & Names

The Performer on a stage,
Falsehood his cage.

The Director in a thirst of control,
Makes superiority his goal.

The Observer humbly let's go,
Tasting the magic of flow.

Without labels and names,
We are one and the same.

08.07.2015 (...)

~ Random ~

In my Bed, She Sleeps

She sleeps tenderly in my bed, spreading herself bare on bedsheets, while her loose hair on the pillow looks like the flow of water, taking it's time to quench the valley's thirst. As a fox, surrounding herself with that furry tail, She pleasures herself in twisting faith, for her body has seen a hundred hunts - tired, weary, scared, yet still strong and unbroken. An expression on her face like that of a dormant bear, sweet and willingly unaware of what is going on outside of her cave.

I ask myself if She realises how She manages to penetrate into my being, fuelling desire, an old territorial instinct of protection, while letting Her roam my bed like a curious new born leopard. I kiss and bite gently her back, as lions in courtship, while with her paws She pulls and pushes me towards her. Her nature is untamed, like that it shall stay, for like a fierce, yet kind and just queen, She has to rule over my bed.

12.07.2015 (morning after an intimate night)

~ Random ~

Never Before

My Beloved,
if what I see is only a glimpse of you,
how vast you must be?!

All that surrounds me aspires to be free,
in living things, I see you looking at me.
I want to reach out my hand and touch your core.
Being in your presence reveals that,
which was never before.

14.07.2015 (interlude of a prayer)

~ Random ~

The Darkness Beneath

She just wishes for someone to hold her hand,
As on the feathered pillow she lays her head.
Waves of curly hazelnut hair covers her face,
While her tongue of those tears has a taste.
Fear of dreaming, those dreams of far away,
Where the dark desolate night rules over day.

Monsters ready to come from under the bed,
She can't let her body cry itself to death.
Yet she finds courage to pray at the Moon,
Whom with His gentle light embraces her in a cocoon.
She dragged out the darkness from beneath,
As she smiles to it with those pearly white teeth.

Light and dark made love, all through the night,
Ending a seemingly eternal fight.

15.07.2015 (a dream that real)

~ Random ~

Drop

A drop just left the cloud in freefall.
On her way down, nearly reaching the surface, she said;
"Will I ever come back up, and lay in your misty embrace once again?"

But it was only when she rippled all over the surface of the lake, that the cloud replied;
"You forgot...that, I am you, as much as, you are me."

18.07.2015 (watching the clouds)

~ Random ~

Rise, Rose, Rise!

You sheltered the soil with your withering petals.
What gave you so much, took all your splendour and joy.
Liked a naked rose, left only with thorns.
Those spines that kept you alive and no one wanted,
Cause only your colour they desired.
Left to die by those you trusted,
Still you held your head up high...high...high...

Waiting for that Moon,
to sing a lullaby...bye...bye...
a forever sleep...sleep...sleep...
It's time...to leave what was behind,
For a new season with a warm breeze is coming...coming...coming,
Once again, you'll be the wildest Rose.
Rise Rose rise!

07.05.2016 (dedicated to a workmate, whom made it all worth it)

~ Random ~

Life in Camera

Sweetly frustrated...
In getting a picture of Her naked.
Like a model She teases,
Hiding under solar white sheets.
Only Her eyes She shows,
With Her ankle She calls.
Some part of me,
Needs Her desperately.
In sugary tears I wait,
Till age becomes late.

24.02.2015 (my perception of Life as a woman)

~ Random ~

Come Time and Again

Hey all of you people that try to understand,
Don't fool yourselves all this will never end.
You will come time and again,
Until you free yourselves from all the pain.
Here you got your Heaven and Hell,
Death, will not come with a tolling bell.
You're trying to save the people that are already free,
Why don't you find for that prison's cell the key?
Got tired and lost in following as sheep,
I just woke up and will never go back to sleep.

16.03.2015 (bringing forth the Revolution)

~ Random ~

Stealing Kisses

They hug each other with a smile on their face,
Giving each other, kisses on the neck while in an embrace.
He grabs her gently by the naked hips,
Pressing her closely to his chest, he wets her lips with his.

"Don't steal kisses!" she said.
"Oh! But I will keep stealing them, until I have drunk all fear." was his reply.

And such he did, for during the night he searched for her in sleep. He found her on a sandy beach playing with waves. Putting two fingers on her fairy lips, he said:

"Can't you hear what these eyes are telling you? What this mouth is begging for? Can't you listen to the rumbling of my heart? Can't you see?
- my Love is free"

23.07.2015 (from a moment of sad departure)

~ Random ~

Magnolian Breeze

After all that suffering and pain...
...She came!

With a magnolian breeze,
She puts me into myself at ease.
Her scarf, a sailing boat roaming the night skies,
Mastering nudity in grace, as a butterfly flies.

26.07.2015 (my first intimate interaction after a hurtful breakup, Dwejra, Gozo)

~ Random ~

The Clouds' Goodbye

What if the clouds would say goodbye!?
Would I still see your face in the sky?
What if the wind finally finds his rest?
Would I still find my way to your mountain crest?
What if the sea stops his kissing flow?
Would my love for you still grow?
- I know that you never come alone,
For...
With your smile comes light,
With your voice comes music,
With your touch comes dance,
With your kiss comes taste,
And with your body comes love...

08.08.2015 (...)

~ Random ~

The Frog's Poison

As a child dwindling on his father's feet,
I listen to stories of heroes venturing beneath.

The eyes drown my sorrow,
In their waters...clear and shallow.

His tongue makes me weightless,
A poison...loving and painless.

The mark of its burning kiss,
Scar my skin in a memento of your lips.

Body bent, but not broken...
A door that is always open.

11.08.2015 (my first experience)

~ Random ~

The Death of Duality

Succumbing to his own pain and misery,
Forgetting Life's magical mastery.
He runs and hides from his nature away,
Accumulating anger and greed on his way.

Waiting for something to set him free,
Killing all that eternally he could be.
Going to work in black bodies bag,
Hailing to the sky his nation's flag.

His favourite game is bloody war,
Death to millions the outcome so far.
Now that his world has stopped turning,
Flames of Love his body is burning!

Nowhere to run, nowhere to hide,
No time for Dr. Jekyll and Mr. Hyde.
As Day is cut by twilight,
Stars dance through the night.

Blood flowing on the Moon's face,
Celebrating the birth of the human race.
The end is near for the torment of duality,
Ending the suffering from personality.

Bringing life to his dreams,
No longer in death he sleeps!

14.08.2015 (…)

~ Random ~

Reflection and Prayer

Our brain perceives all the surrounding environment, and circumstances. Whilst our mind, will taint that view, by judging it from past situations, making them fearful and unwanted.
Our heart sees everything as new. Sometimes it beats gently faster, giving a sweet feeling of anticipation for taste. Just enjoy what your senses gather from around you, with playful innocence.
Make music out of noise, sweetness out of foulness, beauty out of ugliness, fragrance out of staleness.

Make Love out of every touch...

~

I bow to You...
You who have granted me the strength and courage,
to live up to this day.
You adorned my Life with the most precious of jewels,
to them I give no name.
To you, I look from beneath the waters of my eyes and say...
"Kiss me, so that my dream finds its birth!"

~

Don't look too much into books, or too much into preachers and those that name themselves as teachers. You just have to look to the multiplicity of stars, and the luxurious mountain tops, to come to know all there is. You are a birth sprouting from within all that. All is, supporting and loving you. Trust the Divinity that looks at you from behind your own eyes

August 2015

~ Random ~

Your reflection lives on the shimmer of my eyes.
Therefore, you live in me, as much as my heart beats in you.

~ Random ~

Children of Tomorrow

Ice on mountain tops melting into blood,
Under which all Earth will flood.
Angels with wings of gold come to kill,
Those whom with greed make their fill.

Children of tomorrow come out of your grave,
God is dead for those that dare to be brave.
With hair of winds,
and fire in wings...
Beyond Life and Death,
We rise to the eternal breath.

28.08.2015 (...)

~ Random ~

Taken too soon

Dried flowers attached to a street pole,
In remembrance for them that fulfilled their role.

Some say, "they were taken too soon!"
I say, "they wanted to have a closer look at the Moon!"

I shall not grief, for their soul is now in peace,
Their tormented bodies rest at ease.

But I shall live a Life realizing my dreams,
Far away from false prophecies and worldly screams.

"Here" is where all lies and nothing to achieve,
There is no damn reason to ask "what if?"

We are the Dark of Night,
The Shimmer of Light.

03.09.2015 (an observance while driving, Xlendi – Gozo)

~ Random ~

Eternal Kiss

I wish for bliss,
An eternal kiss.

I wish to be alone,
As before I was born.

I wish to be with You,
In an end, never due.

I wish...for Peace, within,
For the glory of Love...
To keep burning!

12.09.2015 (...)

~ Random ~

A Mere Illusion

If Life has no meaning,
Why care so much about a feeling?
Which comes and goes at it's leisure,
Giving no one permanent pleasure.
And if there is a purpose,
Surely, it's not to full our purses.
For the value of money is lack of freedom,
Pushing man to create a selfish kingdom.
Building a Life is a mere illusion,
For it is She that shapes man and gives vision.

14.09.2015 (...)

~ Random ~

Joy and Sorrow

A pain that feels like a hand is squeezing my heart,
as if the breath from my lungs can no longer part.
An angelic melody... tasting of melancholy...
The sweat of her eyes... happiness buys...
On my way to the marriage of Joy and Sorrow,
Through this mystical land as if there is no tomorrow.

23.09.2015 (...)

~ Random ~

Who am I?

Questions that keep breathing,
Answers that never seem arriving.

Will I succumb to a lifeless Life?
Will I rise to a lively Death?

Can you ever penetrate my Soul,
You and me roaming as Whole?

Can you dare my Heart to kiss,
Taint with blood your lips?

Can you take my lungs in your hands,
Take me breathless throughout these lands?

Can I ever shatter the cold mountains of fear,
Conquer their tops, for the world my voice to hear?

To you I now bow and say goodbye...bye...
For my bride has come to take me to the sky.

I will see you all there, beyond hatred and greed,
Whereas one we shall rest, from these chains freed!

24.09.2015 (…)

~ Random ~

Drop of Rain

Haven't I tortured enough my Soul?
Haven't I lived a thousand lives already?
Haven't I become all that I am meant to be?

Therefore, I shall not suffer, nor inflict pain.
I shall live freely and dance as a drop of rain.
She might finally take away all hope,
But I will be no longer tied with a rope.
I know She will come to knock on my chest,
Pressing lightly my lips to her breast.
My body in contentment will die...die..
While my soul is exhaled to the sky!

24.09.2015 (...)

~ Random ~

Fearsome Bird

I don't want nothing except for you to live in me.
For the essential things to rule my Heart, and guide me free!

Just help me to keep the breath of Life alive...
The creature shaped in the form of man to rise,
Like a fearsome bird with flames in His eyes!
The time has come to die and drown in Love,
Shatter this body as I ascend to what is above!

Succumb to the divine,
Have faith, all will be fine . . .

29.09.2015 (...)

~ Random ~

The Aesthetic Beauty

The Heart has been forsaken,
By greed overtaken.
Seduced and imprisoned by all that shines,
To a desolate land in golden chains confined.

I look for Her, but She is nowhere to be seen,
Only during night, we see each other in Dream.

She comes to make love and weep,
Confessing our sorrows in sleep.

In morning two ghostly figures,
Separated by Sea, touching fingers.

10.10.2015 (...)

~ Random ~

Mistress Pain

A humid hole in the ground waiting for its occupant. Morning dew left tears of sorrow on the red roses. Sunlight vainly tries to warm her marble skin. It feels cold. Her eyes still open, yearning for this moment to pass as the clouds make their way. Her lips don't move, yet they plead for a last kiss. I go with my warm hands over her pale body, wishing to arouse once again the life in her. She can't move. Death has taken over. Kissed her eyes while I went with my thumb over her lips.

I nodded to them to gather around, while taking a step back to watch them lower her gently in the ground. We bid each other farewell as She made her way down. She knew that my love for her died the moment she stopped breathing. Silently my mouth whispered a breeze; "Farewell my Pain"

13.10.2015 (a letting go process)

~ Random ~

The Dying Death

The day finally came!

He knew She was waiting for him naked under the bedsheets. Taking a deep breath, he undressed and laid next to Her.

She puts her finger on his mouth compassionately, while he looks at her and gives out a sigh of relief. She kisses his mouth until no life remained in him.

Death is her name,
As the day finally came!

14.10.2015 (a relief from ego)

~ Random ~

Their Friend and Lover

His hate was still echoing in the stone,
Shrieks and weeps that come from bone.
He kept biting at the church's wall,
Wanting in darkness to fall.
Supplicating with threats the sea,
To take his life and not be.

During the night, She kept calling Their names,
Spreading Her wings to burst them in flames!
The desire to lay everything a waste,
Taking away Life's greatest taste.
Making his home, a burnt down land,
Where the air breathes of putrid sulphur sand.

But the Four of them never left his side,
Showing the Devil in him that Love doesn't hide.

19.10.2015 (the first encounter, Comino Island)

~ Random ~

Strawberry Chest

    She saw the world through her chest full of strawberries. Some rotten, others still emitting their blushing smile. It saddened her to see how quickly and violently, the greed of rot could turn everything sour, even the tastiest of fruits. She had no tears left to pour out of her eyes, for all were sacrificed to nourish the fruity bush of berries.

    Hiding behind trees she undressed from the torments of the world. There she stood, laying on the earthly soil, shivering, embracing her legs to her chest as a human yet to be born. To the welcoming night, She said;

"let me wear my Heart on my face, my Soul in my eyes.
I want no more of this human despair, but only to roam the skies."

20.10.2015 (from an interaction with a stranger)

~ Random ~

Taking Flight

As all was preparing for the cold night,
An angel with misty wings takes flight.

He heard my baby's cries,
While praying at the darkened sky.

Wanting for her life to be taken away,
For no longer in pain she wants to stay.

Happiness was only a long-gone memory,
Her heart in soil and stone she did bury.

Hurt by man time and time again,
Love for her has become vain.

With the rape and abuse,
Her soul could no longer fuse.

With her body, finally at rest in the cold night,
She was an angel to the Moon taking flight.

25.10.2015 (from the pain of the feminine)

~ Random ~

Blood of Trees

    A veil of darkness wrapped my heart, shards of torturing glass pierced my eyes, heavy chains pinned me to the ground, condemning me to revolve selfishly on myself. Then, Her voice came echoing through the Earth, the soil was wet in an orgasmic fervour. She appeared to me. Her body in light feathers, wings spanning in the whispering wind. In Her hand a humble cup, filled with the blood of trees. She poured it in my mouth, while Her lips kissed my tongue.

"Let the darkness be your dancer.
Let the light be the music to which you dance.
Let the Love of birth and death be the one who guides your movement.
Let your eyes open as the early sun on ocean waters.
Let the gentle beat of your heart rule over man.
You, that have been bestowed a godly strength, rise!
Wake up to a never ever ending."

25.11.2015 (conceived during a ceremony)

~ Random ~

Selfish Heroin

When his eyes opened to discover Death had his face, they filled themselves with anguished waters. He had to look forcefully into the darkest recesses of his own mind. A veil of dark mist fell, shadowing all that was in sight. His body was fading away, his name and identity were long forgotten. All he felt was the nothingness of separation, the breath that was holding him to the ground was swiping him off his feet, carrying him to a land so known to him. He blissfully closed his eyes, for Death was him.

06.11.2015 (from the remembrance of my heroin days)

~

I have been broken in million pieces, a puzzle with no end. I still remember that bed in the corner of a cell, where my beloved came at night. A maiden with thousand butterflies in hand. Her kiss tasted of blueberries. She told me to dream of a land far, faraway, a place where no one had nothing to say. I am here.

11.11.2015 (from my first encounters with Life while I was in jail)

~ Random ~

*Practice the art,
of an open Heart.*

~ Random ~

Welcome, Grandmother

I know it was time for you to go and rest, but that crack you left in my heart still can't heal itself. It leaks sadness, and like a moving shadow, it makes its way to my throat. A want to cry... but it seems that my eyes had too much of that.

The last time I saw you, your face was bony and pale, your fragile body lying on a cold steel table. I could barely recognise you. But that angel next to you reassured me that he's going to grant you a safe passage, and that for eternity to come, your lifelong tears will be watering my eyes.

If I only was given that wish, that single wish, I would ask to prolong my hand in the unknown and touch your warm hands, those same hands that fed me, carried me, not wanting to let go of me. After having tortured, abused, and imprisoned myself, I have finally grown into a fine man, practicing to be patient, gentle and kind - thanks to the remembrance of you. There are those moments that I look deeply in to my eyes through the mirror, where I can see you in me, with that subtle yet strong voice telling me, "it's ok my boy."

I am embracing that sadness, for it is the lack of your physical presence, and the eternal love I feel for you that gives it Life. I love you, will always do, until the day will come when I will sit again on your lap, while watching the stars and the unfolding of the Universe.

19.11.2015 (remembering my grandmother)

~ Random ~

Be My Friend

All that they did was lie,
Promised us the Moon and his sky.

I don't need a drama queen,
In someone's eyes I want to be seen.

I want someone who can stop this run,
With whom together we enjoy fun.

To be high on Life and wasted,
Wrapped up like kittens in a basket.

I want you to be my friend and let me go,
With those lips, kiss me as the river in flow
.

I want Her to be my summer time girl,
With that red wavy hair in one big curl.

I want Him to be my brother in tears,
In each other our fear disappears.

I want us to unite under one cause,
To not judge, and accept each other's flaws.

What more should I say now?
Except that to you I bow . . .

27.11.2015 (…)

~ Random ~

Prism of Time

She smiled at me from behind that veil of sorrowful clouds.
The purple mist in her eyes was a call for desperate love.
I wished for my hand to grab her pulsating heart,
and quench a lasting thirst with the trickling blood.

Her breasts were youthful,
and in agitation as the restless sea

.

My chest cringing like the earth in quake.

Our bodies were fading away,
as granules of sand in the prism of Time.

28.11.2015 (watching sunset)

~ Random ~

The Ocean of Soul

Lay down next to me,
Beneath warm sheets of sea.

Let the whispering wind weep,
For this secret, I can no longer keep.

I'm going to shed this protective skin,
Since it holds the original sin.

Oh, you make me see, what I thought unreal,
Words escape me in describing what I feel.

I want myself in you to disappear,
As the universe comes to a tear.

Sigh in my ears a lustful lullaby,
Before to this world we say goodbye.

I wish to drown in the oceans of your soul,
While my heart beats for the love of all.

Let's get drunk with the blood of the tree,
In you, I see the divine residing in me.

To kiss those lips and tongue that cannot speak,
Lost between your fingers I no longer seek.

Drink my life and take me away,
In you I will forever stay.

04.12.2015 (watching stormy seas)

~ Random ~

The Fire between Us

In the dark of night, I looked for the first time in her eyes. Her face shone brightly and wildly from the burning fire that was between us. Eyes deep as the abyss itself...to no end...to no beginning. My heart raced as if by Death chased, and Time discovered that he didn't exist at all...in himself he was lost.

"So, do you believe in magic?" she asked.

"What is all this, if not magic?" I replied while looking at the starry night.

The moon was just a silvery sliver in the darkness, as was her smile, put on her face purposely by that God to entertain my imagination. For her words came out from her mouth like the hush hush of grass, a thief of kisses in the night. I forgot, I was fading away in disappearance, this body was there, but I couldn't feel it. All I remember is, that it was dark, burning, infinite, silent, intense, blinding, eternally loving . . .

15.12.2015 (first encounter with a stranger, WhyNot? Vortex, Mqabba)

~ Random ~

The Ascension

    There She stood at the edge of a killer cliff. Waves fought each other, crushing with land to eat her away. The salty rush of sea adorned her, as diamonds on bronze skin. Hundred coloured butterflies with flattering wings, hung to her scarlet ropes of hair. The breeze...the breeze...coming up her feet, carrying a song of resurrection. Dressed only in a spiralling cloud, she held in her hand an immortal kiss. Blood trickled gently down her lips, for there She held an undying rose.
    Next to Her, thousand and one blades of flame, taking away the life out of the serpent in its lair. Falling stars, cut right through the blackened sky in celebration of a forgiving time. And there She was...is...forever will be, saving man from the chains of hopeless wait.

15.10.2015 (seeing a stranger dance, Bubble Festival, Ghajn Tuffieha)

~ Random ~

Don't Wait

At the break of Dawn, on her way to the sea,
as She closed the door behind...She sighed;

"Leave that heart of yours open for me, for I will come again tonight. But don't wait for me. Let my kiss make you awake!"

23.12.2015 (a departure)

~ Random ~

Four Seasons

For Her lips taste like Spring,
with sweet words in bloom.

Her skin carries the salty fragrance of Summer,
with its glittering shine of the warm sea.

Her eyes shine as Autumn melancholy,
with its trees in blazing brown.

Her hair twisted and long as the Winter fields,
with its trails of fields in flowery green.

Meticulously she painted Herself in my heart,
with those thin and caring fingers...
for the Life She proudly carries, has cast a spell on me.

06.01.2016 (from my relationship with Life)

~ Random ~

Prostitute

You on put that short skirt,
Unbuttoned shirt showing your breasts.
Face by heavy makeup hidden,
But your pain cannot be forgotten.

Making it to the streets,
To buy your daily fix.
Selling your sacred body,
To sustain an endless folly.

Society calls you a whore,
Not knowing the child, you never bore.
Eyes looking at you in disgust,
Just to hide their own lust.

I can't stand seeing you in misery,
Having sex with men forcefully.
Oh, my girl can't you see,
That it's time to set yourself free?!

09.01.2016 (…)

~ Random ~

Unveil the Mystery

Oh Love, you smile as if you know,
That someday all this will be gone.

Ours is a story yet to be written,
Thanks to which sin will be forgiven.

Covet that unborn child in your womb,
For he will heal our scars and wounds.

Oh Love, show me to what you're holding on?
Those roses, next to each other they've now grown.

I'm not talking about a childish game,
Love is where one loses his name.

I know, I know, I know it's hard to let go,
Just let the blood of the Earth in you flow.

Come out of the shadows and secrecy,
Take my hand and let's unveil the mystery!

10.01.2016 (...)

~ Random ~

Sober Love

She looks at me with one eye hidden in the shadows of soul,
from within the depth of all that is silent,
and the other in the discovery of Sun, Earth and wild flowers.

Hand in hand we have been in adventurous walks,
exploring each other bodies through valleys of creation,
and up the hilltops of love making.

With the innocence of a child...
We search through each other's hair the mystery.
Licking each other's skin, we get to taste unconditioned life,
swimming the ephemeral shores in the nakedness of the eye.

Drunk beyond any reasoning mind,
we found clarity and sober Love.

17.01.2016 (relating with Life)

~ Random ~

Soul in Man

She calls upon my name,
And I succumb to her game.
One of everlasting desire,
An inferno of fire.

She tells me to love her,
And I am the one to dare.
Above sheets of cloud we play,
Naked from masks is the only way.

She says that, to her love I have to be true,
So that as one, the illusion we break through.
I forgave who I was and am,
A Soul in a mere man.

23.01.2016 (relating with Life)

~ Random ~

October Rain

She falls upon my body as the fresh October rain.
Each drop quenches the thirst of desire,
after the nakedness of Summer.

For I became submissive towards Her...
and like the flowing long hair that adorns all that She is,
I am nothing but a glimmer of the precious stones that fill Her crown.

Love has taken me by surprise,
and bare from all possessions,
I have to be to receive it.

Yet, it is not in my body that I hold it,
for I am nothing but...
the vanity of all the beauty that surrounds me.

26.01.2016 (the greatness of Life)

~ Random ~

Bring Forth your Soul

    A gentle sound of fingers on piano keys. The fragrance of fields covered with dew, fills the air. In a cup of black coffee I find the love She treasures for me. An untamed aroma lingers between us, forging transparent paths, which one can only follow with heart.
    She asks as her fingers still the piano strike;
"What am I to you? What have you seen in me that I can't see?"

And I reply with a slight smile;
"Your body was shaped in a way to turn black and white in grey.
With eyes coloured as the infinite dark and light skies,
lingering clouds gazing upon me from afar.
That long hair ever falling into an eternity of opportunities,
upon which I lay my face to get lost.
I see in you the greatness, an undying relentlessness…
I can feel your heart in weep, when your body is in sleep…
My soul aches for you to be free, as you are a reflection of me."
"You are to me all that there is to see. The unwavering force of the universe. That spirit dancing in winds. The shaking of trees praising all there is to be. Well, you are to me the death of words, all that that cannot be understood by reasoning. You are fields of flowers in bloom, the movement of the heart in its beat. Call me crazy, call me wanderer, call me a dreamer. Call me whatever you want, because it just won't change no thing, because this is no fling!"

Her fingers now laid still, on a piano that became mute. Sound was deaf. Only the violent glaze of tears now ruling her eyes were on stage, realizing that fear was only keeping her in a cage.

"Lay upon me my love, bring forth your soul…"
She said.

27.01.2016 (relating with Life)

~ Random ~

The Defeated Heroin

It pierced my flesh with an orgasmic pleasure, in the wait for blood to appear. While plunging into my body I could feel myself fading away, and the sweet release from the pain, as the shivers stopped with a rush of tingling warmth. Each breath felt like the last, married with the wish of a disappearing death. I prayed upon you to receive the stranger that has become me. With eyes glazed in the mirror I stared, in the vain hope to find a shimmer of light.

But night had fallen, and with it the Moon drowned in clouds of despair.

"I search for you in the mirror, but I can find no more,
All I can remember is your fragile body all bloody and sore.
Oh, help me love...oh my kin please help yourself,
Let me kiss your bruised skin as the shores and surf.
I know we roamed together the streets,
In search for that dreamy welcoming fix.
Oh, help me love...I am here to greet you,
Loose those masks that made your body blue.
Please don't leave me now brother,
For there is life for you out here."

27.01.2016 (in remembrance)

~ Random ~

Love is Change

Love...love is change.
Love is the air we breathe...
it goes out as it comes in,
but it's undying fragrance lingers.

The taste of Love resides in a memory that never dies,
taking you to places beyond reasoning.
For Love, cannot be understood, contained, or tamed.

Sometimes it is like a balloon,
you have to let go of the string,
that binds it to your hand.

Love is work, and it takes heart, because the mind tries hard to
stay away from it.
And what is sorrow, if not an expression of the love we long for?
Love...Love is change.

28.01.2016 (...)

~ Random ~

Valley of Yearning

Oh, my Love, what is this that is tearing us apart?
Was is my birth, the first dawn of this beating heart?

They told us that we have sinned before the breath,
But isn't that infernal desire which drives the World?

As a hollow reed in the Valley of Yearning I will bend,
With the wind, I give myself to what the ancients sang.

Have not my trickling tears looked upon thyself,
Lost would have been the memory of when we met.

If they could only know the softness of your kiss,
Made of Sorrow and Joy, are those moisten lips.

Drifted off has the fear of them calling me insane,
For one day, they will realize the greatness of your name.

30.01.2016 (from my longing for Love)

~ Random ~

Life, will begin the moment you find yourself alone.

~ Random ~

The Awakened Man

He has awakened in the name of Love,
to wage wars, hurricanes and storms.

In his touch, He is gentle as the bee on flower,
yet in his will, there is power.

He is meant to write songs in Her name,
but with blood plays the game.

In love-making, not with promises He greets,
but with lustful grinning teeth.

He longs for Her as the chase of the Moon,
and so, for Her in his heart He makes room.

He doesn't call himself divine, nor holy,
for that, will only fuel the egoic folly.

He is just a man that walks the land,
whom with fairness takes Her in hand.

30.01.2016 (…)

~ Random ~

"Do I deserve to be loved?"

With a cigarette in hand, he let himself ask the question; "Do I deserve to be loved?"

No one was around to reply the question, except for Shadows and Fumes. Shadows was the first to reply;
"I am colourless, and sometimes I even feel lifeless. Shall I hate you for that? I start from the edge of your body, extending far beyond reach. I am created by your marriage with Light, and from you I take my different shapes and forms. I can say that thanks to Light, you create me. Shall I not love you for that? Although you made me colourless, I feel your urge to drown in me. And for all that I do love you."

Meanwhile Fumes, like an ethereal snake dancing in mid-air, blanketed the room. In his reply, there was no urgency;
"From your lungs, I transpire. By your breath, I am given life. And although you know that I cause harm in your body, you still love the taste of me, while romanticizing with my exhale. You wish no end to me. Shall I not take pride in this display of your twisted love? I purposely fill up the space, so all that, which is invisible becomes for you tangible. That it is the only way that I know how to humbly repay you, just to show you that I love you."
Silence fell, and as his eyes were closing with exhausted tiredness, their last words echoed into his being...
"We accept and surrender to our Selves, for your will upon us is absolute...and to that we bow in gratitude, for You are the greatness we reflect."

Note: all of us have at some point, felt the greatness of pure Love. Some of us get sad, because they see themselves not deserving of such, and keep on wondering about. Others even reject it although it is what they wish for. All of us have come a long way for this

~ Random ~

moment in time. Choices done, and promises broken. Consciously, or unconsciously, we have been writing our story all along. It is for that reason, that we are deserving of all that we are surrounded, within and without.

You can't be me, and I can't be you. Yet, we all can come to love each other understandingly, after we have come to love ourselves. You can't be nothing else, but this. Trying, will only cause suffering. You are what you always wished for. You just have to come and see it. Trust Life. Trust yourself, and be the recognition of how perfect all is.

You are perfectly enough!

~

"As there is the rainbow after the storm,
and the butterfly that was once a warm...
You already are who you want to be,
No need to fight in order to be free.
Within our desire, we don't transform,
For out of this Life we are born.
Let Life steal away your heart,
For this is a never-ending path."

31.01.2016 (from a conversation among friends)

~ Random ~

Shakti

With stars protecting my numbing sleep,
I flow through Love's gentle stream.

I feel Her presence waiting for me to wake up,
Holding the Universe within a humble cup.

Oh, Shakti I hear your voice...
From the shadow that crawls,

To the eternal dance, I will rise,
While losing my fears in your eyes.

Yearning the gates of desire and faith,
But for now, I am patiently in wait...

02.02.2016 (for the dancer of LIFE)

~ Random ~

Born out of this World

I have lived for millennia by the semen of desire,
in its urgent seeking of the universal womb,
for an experience of flesh.

Chest filled with yearning for love,
the mirroring pool,
whom gentle ripple takes the ocean in storms.

I seek, and quest through the hearts and love of man,
for in Her hand I am only a pen,
going between lines and pages as fields of vine.

Her beauty I shall ponder,
where my eyes the clouds wander.

Thoughts are just the being at play...
From the aroma of fond memories,
to the eternal dance of sexual pleasures,
with the dancer of eternal treasures.

Who am I...
if not a Soul, whom this World a child bore?

06.02.2016 (for existence)

~ Random ~

SHE *(in relation to LIFE)*

What follows is a series of poems and texts, that came to me in the span of few months, one after the other. There was none, and as such it came to be that I was relating to LIFE, with every figment of my imagination and being.

I am blessed, because from my home I can witness sunrise easily every morning. It is that scene, of this ball of fire rising from above the horizon, that has fuelled most parts of these texts. For me, that moment when Day sheds its light upon the Night, is like being born again. Leaving the dark waters of the womb, to emerge within the breath of this world.

To these texts, I haven't given a name or a title, for nothing in them is deserving of that.

~

Upon Her lips, falls the nectar of death,
such sweetness one can only taste once.
She hides Her nakedness behind clouds,
shaking off stars from Her hair.
Waves in elegant fury have shaped Her body,
spiders weaved Her skin in silk.
In my yearning, I desire to touch that intangible form,
for I wonder about what it is,
that can contain such mesmerizing beauty.
Only She, manages to capture it all inside.
The way She moves, feet not touching the earth...
With a voice that echoes in whirling winds,
catching my Soul in an everlasting fire.

08.02.2016

~ Random ~

SHE *(in relation to LIFE)*
cont…

I wake up at the first hint of dawn.
Her light has already seen through me.
She blows gently at the leaves on trees,
soaking the soil with tears of Night.
My eyes are starting to surrender of ever seeing Her.
Yet She speaks to me, in million different tongues,
extending Her hand for the dance that I feared for so long.
I doubt if I will ever come to know Her,
for She is spread in thousand and one pieces all over the land.
While I am in a vain quest to capture this Beauty,
She has fiercely awakened the sleeping Death within me.

10.02.2016

~

With a hand on my chest, and the other drowning in sheets if soil,
eyes fill themselves with tears, and body aches in sorrow…
I pray for you to love me once more.
In trying to understand my desire,
I implore silence to speak to me with his deafening tongue.
Pieces of me sit as seeds on flowers,
whose time has come to be blown away by the cold breeze of sea.
In that drop of dew, that lingers eternally in the bottomless depths
of Soul,
I see the universal marriage of Blood and Earth.
Such is the greatness you have bestowed me with, my Beloved.
And as your fingers go through my hair bidding me farewell…
I find peace in being just a man.

11.02.2016

~ Random ~

SHE (in relation to LIFE)
cont...

There is a yearning to roam the female body,
in its splendour and dullness,
with its gentleness of touch and sharpness of birth.
Yet I fear misunderstanding, the loss there is in lust,
the coming to forgetfulness of thy Self.
Every form of art that transpires to me speaks of Her,
of the unexplainable beauty, which with genius, shapes the curves and forms,
folded in sweet textured tapestries of pale and tanned skin.
So, I shall ponder Time, and ask Him of how all this came to be,
to that moment when the Eye started to see.

11.02.2016

~

It was Summer,
with his sweat dripping skin that got into my dreams.
He reminded me of her playfulness,
and how She manages the tides of sea.
On tip-toes, She crosses the beach of sand in a spiralling dance,
as if She was jumping from flower to flower, and from star to star,
making her way through space and time in a motionless wave.
I don't know if She knew I was there,
looking at the beauty She was transpiring,
with eyes gleaming in tears by the shallow waters.
For sure before She left, She did whisper some words,
" ... "

17.02.2016

~ Random ~

SHE *(in relation to LIFE)*
cont...

There will be one day where She will happen as dawn,
shattering the Night, illuminating the skies such as to the stars will cease to appear.
She will rob me of my clothes and I of her sorrow,
and nothing will stop the march of desire.
For I crave Her, but Her thirst for me is greater.
I will tear off thorns, as she makes our home Her throne.
Yet Her strength lies in taming the wild within Her,
for She can be sophisticated but not domesticated.
We will lose each other in lust, as the sea's horizon that disappears in the skies.
The selfish seeking for other lovers will stop, as one Moon and one Sun.
We will recognise each other by the pain we bore,
now a distant memory reminding us of how Love "is the more."
Such is, the come to happening of Man and Woman.

11.02.2016

~

In those eyes, I see the Universe in dance,
the constellations of stars in a hurricane frenzy.
A well, that drowns in its depth of infinite waters.
Formless clouds, that bring in togetherness,
the marriage of Dusk with Dawn.
I am but the Moon, reflecting your beauty,
where in my simple Heart, your greatness I behold.

12.02.2016

~ Random ~

SHE *(in relation to LIFE)*
cont...

Life's journey became lighter, when I started to express what I feel.
Giving life to feelings, letting them bloom as wild flowers in the
valley of ecstatic sexuality. I see All in a constant kiss, such as the
roots that penetrate the soil, the clouds in mist covering with
jealousy the naked Earth, the sea courting restlessly with his
lustful waves the shore. While singing, and telling to me...
"Thy liberation lies in giving what you have away; from feelings, to
the illusionary substance of materialism. Such is the becoming to
Light, within this human journey."

18.02.2016

~

A Soul pushes Her lips to mine,
In a burning kiss, sweet as wine.
With Her eyes on fire and body in a hellish desire,
She says;
"To you I open the Valley of Thirst,
where you shall get lost in birth.
Drink and be drunk of me.
Make love, and succumb to me.
For I am You, in the never ending!"

01.03.2016

~ Random ~

SHE *(in relation to LIFE)*
cont...

From within the soil, She raised herself, and said:
"Unto you I dispel my pale body, void of all, for you to write upon.
Turn around the hills of my breasts with a feathered pen,
and sink your desire in the valleys of my legs.
We will merge with a heavenly death and dissolve into one.
To you, I shall bear wisdom with a violent birth in fields of cotton.

Extend your hands, and hold in them my beating heart.
Look upon my eyes and linger there.
Know, that all you see, and don't...is you!"

06.03.2016

~

Her hair smells like the Moon with its silver shine.
Her skin tastes like the morning mist that covers the fields.
With a gracious face adorned with the biggest pair of wild eyes,
always lost in their stare, She asks;
"what do you see, when you look at me?"

"I look at you and marvel.
I ponder about the architect of such a creation.
Your voice is as violent as the flight of a butterfly.
You move like the clouds in the sky, with their furious calmness,
and void of purpose. Yet, I close my eyes and find you there, in all
your majesty and poverty,
resting in all that is."

06.03.2016

~ Random ~

SHE *(in relation to LIFE)*
cont…

Thousand one faces hiding in rain drops,
surrounding me with sorrowful laughter.
Into me they go for their descent of love,
only to engage in a conversation of loss.
A river of emotions, burdens my soul, heavy,
yet sweet in its melancholy.
She sits next to me on the edge of my heart.
Together we recite tales of lovers,
who made it to the infinite grounds of unending desire.

09.03.2016

~

As the Night, gently, and seductively sets herself in…
I cannot help but wonder if I will find her again,
in my dreams and in my bed, under starry sheets.
Some nights I hear her words coming in whispers,
in marriage with that warm breath on my neck.
She feathery drifts me to lands built on clouds,
where the Moon sings a serenade of long forgotten times.
A lullaby for Lovers;
"Truthful to his heart, he sees Her as equal,
and adores her nature, for She is the one that gives Him birth.
In return, She reveres Him for his strength and loyalty,
for He is the ground beneath her feet."
…that is how it goes in dream.

09.03.2016

~ Random ~

SHE *(in relation to LIFE)*
cont...

At times, She comes adorned with butterflies, stars, and dressed in clouds.
Other times like today, She comes dressed in rags, and suffering famine.
"What can I do?", I ask.
With her muffled voice, She replies; "As I am, you shall take me.
For this day and the coming night, we shall be poor, and walk in the midst of man's sorrow."

11.04.2016

~

    With her dress of dark thick green leaves, She came to take all with her. I could see the skies fighting amongst them, for a mere glimpse of her eyes. Fireflies would surround her steps, sinking softly into the ground, with flowers blooming with everyone. She knew so well what troubles man, and in all glory, She wanted to elevate that sorrow, to the highest form of joy. She knew the voice of the Heart's pulse, its yearning, and melancholy. She knew it as a mother bearing her first child, for She was born out of that same seeking.

    It was the Unknown that held her pace, and the marriage of Sun and Moon held light upon her face. She bowed to man, with the same compassion that the giver offers the beggar. It was then, that She clothed man with her own skin, baptizing him with a kiss that held no time. In her desire, She wished for man to make a bed out of his own misery, so to lay upon, and watch the stars in dance.

    For him to remember, and not to forget...home!

20.04.2016

~ Random ~

SHE *(in relation to LIFE)*
cont...

I look at All forgetting where my being ends.
There I can see Her on the butterfly's wings,
with a smile of a thousand gazes in winds.
She takes my hand before the deep fall into Love.
So, looking at the night sky I wonder;
"What would it be like...to take our intimacy to the stars?"

27.04.2016

~

Face half covered with a scarf, and eyes peeping out to the world.
Her lips smile, like the new moon, that falls in love with his own reflection
on the face of the sea.
Her shyness covers a world full of mystery,
of whispering winds in lonely deserts,
and mystic lamps, with genies in orgies.

Come, and let me know more of who you are...
of how you lay your head on your pillow at night...
of how your cheeks blush and eyes wonder in all their shyness...
of how your lips bite each other in desire.
Show me, you!

01.05.2016 (LIFE from a girl)

~ Random ~

SHE *(in relation to LIFE)*
cont...

She rises again from the death of thousand nights,
Bearing no memory of the sleepless and darkened skies.
The sea veils her virginity with translucent glare,
For kings, had bowed for that hand in marriage.
She strips off them the riches stolen from humanity,
Leaving them witness of their own greed and vanity.
One can meet Her at the break of dawn,
Together with the moon, in a loving moan.

31.07.2016

~

On Her way to sleep, She left sprinkles of light in clouds...
for me to follow, and find Her in all nakedness, under bedsheets of
sea and stars.

So, I knocked at her ageless doors, and She opened.
I was a hungry, and She fed me the most fulfilling seeds.
I was thirsty, and She brought me the sweetest of waters.
I was a beggar, and She bathed me,
and gave me to wear humble cloths.
But first, I had to strip from myself,
all the glistening silver and gold.
Only then, I was able to enter the gardens that led to her home.

19.08.2016

~ Random ~

SHE *(in relation to LIFE)*
cont...

I never saw someone carrying so much wilderness with elegance and grace. She would innocently smile at you, and your breath would go deaf. If you catch Her occasionally staring, wondering at the night sky, your heart would blush. Few fortunate ones have seen her dance, and they all lusted after Her. Seduced by the thought of bedding Her, they went fruitlessly in hunt, only to succumb to their own desire.

For Thunder was the guardian that looked after Her, and Fire was the one upon whom She walked. Mankind always wanted to possess Her, only to kill himself in the quest.

So let me dig my own grave, and abandon me to the hands of Destiny. Let Dawn gift me with the Light that shall bring forth the sweetest of Deaths. For I know, that when my eyes will close, She will come...as the pulse that enters the new-born.

27.09.2016

~

She was decaying with every photograph, yet their obsession made them oblivious to Her, ever getting close to death. Her immortality was slowly being eaten away by every capturing shot. Stripped moments of eternity, portrayed on cheap paper. The grandiosity of Love displayed cheatingly as two lovers kissing.

We have become masters of "fake", where only few manage to stay truthful to the promise done upon birth. The journey of Life's self-discovery is veiled with the illusory, and seductive belief of "who we are".

21.07.2016

~ Random ~

SHE *(in relation to LIFE)*
cont...

    It's not always easy to come back from the land of sleep. Finding a tongue that has bled out of words, I let myself listen to Her songs. Covered with a blanket of fierce colours, and seductive mist, She dares me to enter.
    Skin laced with honey, legs open as valleys, breasts top Her body as eager hills... is how She welcomes any man, who awakens to her call.
    I shall let her voice embrace me as a dancing whip.
I shall journey time and Suns, so to lay hopelessly at each other's feet. I shall cradle our daughter, and sing to her of the Moon and his nights.
We shall make Love, upon the seeking of mankind.

02.10.2016

~ Random ~

SHE Alone! *(in relation to LIFE)*

She is alone in her wandering of the clouds and stars. With two feet that dance her body in ways unimaginable to man. One hand carries the seeds, while the other blows them gently over the Earth. She sows the fields with great care, weaving them with colours like a knitted garment, as her lips call upon the butterflies and bees, to proliferate Life with their shimmering wings.

The Wind is helpless against the tender multiplicity of her hair. He goes through each one, infinitely seduced by the length of such silky strings, running from her head, down her back, and up again to meet the Sun. Yet, in no instance, this veil of glistening strings covers her face, it just tends to her defining body of splendour and nakedness.

I have seen Her not in my dreaming nights, but at the first sight of Dawn...in that waking state between Death and Life. Never have I managed to touch her skin, because like water, my hands can't hold upon them, the great eternal Movement. Not yet, at least. But my eyes have been bestowed to me for that purpose, to gaze into Hers. It is when my hands start to go through air and paper, finding harmony with words...where letters become sound.

It was just this morning, that the hills led me to a secret only few know;

"Part-take in Life as the Sea with the Shore,
have none, and yet seek all.
Let your Heart be unburdened from desire.
Find that silent Space within you.
Let you comfortably lay upon emptiness.
Alone you must learn to be.
There, She will come...not for you...
but to be one with the Love within you."

22.01.2017

~ Random ~

*Even the fragility of a butterfly can overthrow,
and cast an endless shadow.*

~ Random ~

The Rabbit Hole

I woke up embraced by my own fear,
with a mouth in foul taste and sheer.
A fire so cold taking wind within my soul,
wondering what is it, He's looking for.
A despairing question resounds in my ears,
cutting through my skin as a spear.

"Who am I?", asks the Waker...

...as soon as he forgets his past of Sleeper.
A riddling story of confusion with thoughts in whore,
taking me down the rabbit hole.

09.03.2016

She has had many names, infinite faces, and ageless colours. Her departure, always leaves some emptiness, and I am left again, clearing the cob webs from my own lack of self-love. It is in that time of "once again", where I meet the faithful companion, who never left my side.

Since child, I have always looked in the mirror, trying to see His face. But all I could see, was an actor with a number of false names. It is "here", where I keep realizing that;

He is unborn...unseen...the unmanifested, infinite Love!
Maybe that it is why, I am sometimes forgetful of Him. Could it be that, that is the reason why I keep seeking a companion of flesh? "Forgetfulness"?

Yet...this warmth, and dance of pulses, has made all of this,
worthwhile...with this "Other", never leaving my side.

08.08.2016

~ Random ~

I have tried a million times over, and crossed hundred deserts. I have strayed far and wide, tainting bodies with needles and bruises. I have dug deep graves in the heights of the tallest mountain, fighting dreams of ridicule. Smoked 600 lives within the singularity of a breath, and plucked 99 feathers for never written love letters, while cutting down lives as straws, and seeing thunder falling as dominoes. Have my world gone fake for the 21st time, I would have resurrected it till the never-ending.

For I have drowned myself in sorrow, wept in loneliness and greed. I have lusted after the knees and lips of women, till Death came and made love to me.

I am all that I am within the marriage of what is sacred and profane...the depth of your hunger, and the spitefulness of sufficiency. I am what you will never understand. All that which is above the horizon, and beyond the abyss. I am what will grant your wishes, and give life to your dreams. I am the aging youth and the birth of the old man.

I am you!

11.11.2016

~ Random ~

Transcending Heroin

Well, I don't know how many of you ever asked the question; "Who am I?"

Since I was a kid I couldn't relate with my name, my voice, my face and body. All I could relate to, was this inner intelligence that took me to faraway places. But growing up, I felt it as a burden. I couldn't express what I felt, otherwise people would think I am crazy...at least that is what I thought.

I would look to the sky with such intensity that I would get lost day-dreaming in the ecstatic feeling of nothingness. I saw the motion of everything. People birthing, and dying didn't make any difference for me. They both were a celebratory act of Life, from Life itself. But at one point I couldn't distinguish between the nightmare and the dream. I saw everything collapsing around me, belief systems, realities...nothing stuck.

As I felt myself falling, I grabbed a life line, the only one I saw. It was heroin, the famous opiate that numbs mind, body and spirit. Believe it or not, the three of them stop the functioning. Awareness becomes no longer present as their guidance.

But well, amazing things are happening thanks to that experience. I've dug such a deep hole, that now, it has been filling itself with the water that quenches the thirst of reason. For everything is what it is, bound to change and love, because one cannot exist without the other.

This inner intelligence, if we listen to it attentively, and heed to Its volition, it will bring us to know ourselves. We will come to know that, "We are it!"

We are the Love we yearn for.

18.02.2016

~ Random ~

Overdose

Yes, it was light, warm, and night.

They have told me so much, and so repeatedly of that place. Yet, it was nothing at all as they have described it, and not even close to what I have imagined. I went there through a quite unusual entrance. All I remember was the prick of a needle, blood mixing itself so ferociously with the murk, warmth, haze...daze... exit...enter.

A numb body in flight, having nothing in sight.
The echoing sounds, had no bound.
I forgot all and my name, it was an end to the game.

First thing I reckoned was, a wetness around my hip, and neck area. My eyes were slow to open, while my ears came alive from a distance. The first sight was that of my car in vertical position. A sense of comfort came into me with that familiar sight, because my car was the place I called home. No matter where I was, alone with the brown powder, or having wasted sex with a girl...in it, I felt like a dominant ruler, and hellishly safe.

But the faraway cold voices, started to get nearer, disturbing the white warmth I was in. Their hands, smelling of surgical elastic gloves, were touching my body and face, taking me from the cloudy grass I laid upon, to a hard, and unwanted surface. I could see feet surrounding me, some dressed in white, and others in dark blue. Only then, I had a full recognition of what had happen.

With a sensation of an invading tube in my hands, I tried to get myself in the car...to switch on some music, so that everything will be ok. It worked most of the time. To drown myself and all the pain, in that ocean of electronic sounds, vibrating basses, and eclectic voices. Yet, my strength hadn't fully faded in, so gently they laid me in the back of an ambulance.

~ Random ~

That was my first overdose. After that, I would inject myself not for the high, but to experience again death. The year I don't remember. What I do remember is the loving friend who I was with. Without his intervention, most probably I won't be writing these words, nor I would have known so many beautiful people, nor I would have met such wonderful women, that thought me intimacy, playfulness, compassion, selfless sex, and longing. Nor I would have come to make peace with my family, and myself.

Thank you loving friend...to you I owe a Life, and all that came after.

24.01.2017 (a recollection)

~ Random ~

Is It?

Love...

How many times I have asked myself and wondered about the meaning of this word? Countless for sure. Lately I was caught up in another web of illusion, where Love was seen as this hippie free for all loving state of affairs. Seeking at one go more than one lover, with the selfish belief that I was spreading "love" here and there, like some magic fairy dust, culminating the pair in an orgasm. Well, realization is sometimes a tough pill to swallow, because down with it goes our pride, as shit down the shitter.

Society created the delusional belief of the "right one", just to keep feeding the illusion we already live in. What is good for me today, can be poisonous tomorrow...those that one fine day discover that, what they have been eating, was just killing them faster, surely can vouch for this. All is in change. Who I was yesterday, is no longer today.

So how can we think, that we can live with "and they lived happily ever after" motto, if we hold on to things and concepts?

In every affair, there will be ups and downs, and to go through them one has to practise acceptance and surrender towards oneself and others. If after trying all that, you still feel it is not working, then it is time to let go...hold on to no-thing and flow!

Love is the coagulated blood under the skin that forms bruises. Love is the earth in quakes, opening up huge spaces on the face of the land just to create the right environment for new species to thrive. Love is the hardship we face just till we learn that so needed lesson. Love is not bound only to man/woman, man/man, woman/woman. Love is the lioness in hunt, sinking its claws in the prey, to feed its cubs. Love is the black widow that kills its mate, just to have enough energy in harnessing its eggs. Love is not free, but freedom. Love needs work, work on oneself, first and foremost. Love is the flow of water, dragging everything with it to the

~ Random ~

godliness of the ocean. Love is the hawk in its flight, and the wind under its wings. Love can be Death when it comes to reclaim the life of the sufferer. Love is when night meets day, and day fades in night. Love is the Darkness in ecstasy with Light.
    Everything has purpose, to serve in our growth as human beings. Getting us more and more conscious of our actions and patterns. Love will swipe you of your feet, either with a gentle breeze or with a hurricane wind.

Love happens, where duality ends.

13.02.2016

~

Love is Selfish

As the tree absorbs water to strengthen its roots, and harden its trunks, before it can bear any fruit...so do we, have to take care, and put our health and happiness first and foremost. Only then, the by-products of Love, such as; relationships, and friendships, can have a place of truth in our lives.
Come to love your Self unconditionally, be fully human and fully divine.

25.02.2016

~ Random ~

Set It Free

Relationships are one of the hardest things to build, and even harder to let go of. For some reason, it doesn't occur to us that things change. We get lost, while riding the "good" wave, in thinking that we have finally found stability, and security. But was goes up has to come down.

Flowers die, and yet they multiply.
Butterflies ravish the air with their wings,
yet they don't think what tomorrow will bring.

Let them roam the fields of Love within your Heart,
but away from the chains of attachment.
Allow your Love for them, to change, and bloom in the eternal plains within your Self.
Don't try to contain it, and lock it away in memories...for it is restless and magical.
Don't suffocate and kill, all that your Heart holds dear.
If you love someone, set them free.

29.06.2016

~ Random ~

The Wind's Breath

Love, is the Wind's breath beneath my wings,
As the Sun that dances with Clouds in rays sings.

Observing my own judgements and beliefs,
Makes the Heart from enslavement freed.

In the eternal Voice, we will get lost,
As questions stop being imposed.

Oh my Love, whose lips taste of bliss,
I know your nectar I will forever kiss.

21.02.2016

~ Random ~

Aya

She's near, and I can feel it.

My stomach twists in anticipation. Those butterflies, have now become eagles soaring over the valleys of my womb. Skin feels cold, for it trembles with own insecurities and fear of loss.
I have visited her house more than once now, but each time feels different, not knowing how and with what She will welcome me. It is not enough, that I enter her temple naked. I have to shed the masks I myself have engraved on my face. The illusion I've built and believed, has to die, for me to be re-born into a world of souls hiding in withering bodies.
I see that we have become too attached to our body and its cravings, and for us to live fully, and in unconditioned Love, that attachment has to die.
I can see Her in the distance, cup in hand, hair full of coloured feathers. Big wild eyes, full of the lust that man seeks. Skin, adored with the rays of dawn, and a mouth spilling with water of wisdom that will make you forget thirst.
To Her I say; "I will stare upon your eyes as I bow to you, so to surrender my fragile mortality. With you I shall rise from my own ashes and shadows, for I will give birth to my Self in an inferno of flames. We shall make love upon the despair of man, so that all will come to know, that nothing was and everything is!"

14.03.2016 (days before a ceremony)

~ Random ~

Natem

She lays in graciousness at the edge of my sleep, with eyes that illuminate the night...while I live dreams of longing...only to rest in the depths of own desire.

To my sorrow, I have only seen shades of Her at the break of dawn,
just to disappear as mist over the wet fields.
And so, I shall wait, at the doors of my heart,
where I will ask the Moon for her hand in marriage,
while Wind whispers to me her name...

"Natem"

20.03.2016 (during a ceremony)

~ Random ~

Golden Grain

They shall give you a name to call you by,
Which will make you forget, you who truly are.

At night, you will rest your head on my chest,
And I will fill your dreams, with arousing breaths.

On beds of sandy dunes, we will lay for love,
As the jealous Moon looks from above.

Clouds will gather by, full of thunder and rain,
To bless the sacred seed of golden grain.

But at dawn in your wake, you will go on,
Pretending that you're not scared and all grown.

Just bow down, and look into the watery well,
Deep inside, you will see yourself blooming in there.

15.03.2016 (in relating to myself)

~ Random ~

Morning in Mist

Everything became "short", in the pleasurable experience of her discovery. Suddenly I found my Self on the edge of her legs, going back to the top of her breasts. On every string of her hair, infinite roads, and upon her eyes, waves caressing shores. Prose, recited by her lips in motion, words and Love in fusion. Her kiss licked pain, as fresh water from rain. In finding my body I didn't succeed, for my Soul has been freed.

And so, let me tell you about Her...

"She comes dressed in fireflies,
with wings of hurricanes and stars.
You might think that She doesn't exist,
because She's subtle as Morning in mist.
Her colours your eyes won't catch,
but your mind will try to fetch.
You have to close them,
and feel the growing stem.
She turns realities into symphonies,
merging your Soul with the Whole."

Why not let Her rise from within my dreams?
For She is the place I buried my heart in.

And the dream goes, that...

"While I tend to my field, hands in soil, for the cultivation of Self...
She comes carrying the Unknown, feet not touching the Earth.
Her wild, shy eyes, to my Heart give pulse."

16.04.2016 (conceived in a misty morning)

~ Random ~

Past Revisited

While walking through the streets of my childhood town,
my heart cringed,
eyes blemished with an uprising of tears from within.

Old faces got older, drug users with holes in their eyes,
drug dealers got more tattoos, more gold, and luxurious cars.

A flood of a so well-known energy surrounded me,
they call her Pain.
I invited her to come in, and in an embrace, we made Love.

She didn't know what it was, She just smiled and looked content.

Pain can be our greatest teacher, by embracing it, surrendering to it, and show it Love. It will transform itself into the most wonderful butterfly of Joy.

06.05.2016 (while walking through my birth town)

~ Random ~

Dawn of Awakening

There is no brake pedal to this spiralling Life. There ain't no stopping it!

I don't know which goes faster, the inner or the outer? Can't distinguish one from the other. Emotions dig deep in me, as if they are deriving a sexual pleasure out of it. My mind in its crisis, creates intricate illusions, so that it has something to hold on to. While all my being goes through a constant fall into all that is God, the nothingness...where in its demise the ego grips, and scratches to the walls of fear, that it builds.

No matter what I try to tell myself, no matter what is written in those second-hand experiences on books. No matter what, this rape of reality seems to persist. As I try to surrender, the intensity grows, with my Soul in howl at the New Moon, which slivers the black sky as a thief in the night, with his diamond cutting knife.

"I will fill you up with dreams...
arouse you with desire,
just to take you higher
...and insane.
But only when you are empty of all that,
you, shall enter me."

Oh yes, it is coming! The Dawn of Awakening!

10.05.2016 (from a current state)

~ Random ~

Gods and GOD

What is this dance, that attracts everything to its self,
and opposite?
Dreams of everlasting Love, free from the rape of ravenous cages.
Of man rising above the lust for his own reflection,
Distorted reality written down my pupils, is now scripture.

Electronic beeps, have replaced heart beats.
Radiating screens, fill the void with empty dreams.

Where is my pen?
What's become of my paper?
Has their dance been extinguished?
Have you left me?
Or it was I, that drifted of...slowly, slowly?
Shall I call upon you once again?

God help me remember her name!
She that moved mountains, and danced with clouds, upon whom
all world lies.

Earth...the place where gods are fabricated.
Mechanical gods. Organic gods.
Within such little rock journeying through space, gods become.
There are those that indulge in destruction, and those that divulge
creation.

God...the end of the eternal realization.

21.05.2016 (...)

~ Random ~

The Marriage

What am I, if not...
The gentle breeze, between a forest of trees.
The raging wind, upon the sleeping seas.

The hand of man, touching your pale face.
The marriage of us, within the womb of space.

Come my Love, and rise, from the illusion of illusion.
For although it escapes us, this is, Reality in its fusion.

01.06.2016

~ Random ~

The Second of the Twelve Commandments

2. You shall not make false idols.
- Don't put your faith in other people's hands. The Truth in you, contains all that the scriptures fail to put in words. In trying to understand other people's path, you're losing your own, for the Heart knows, where the mind distorts. No preacher, no scripture, and no law is above you. Your Life is your own to live, while respecting others as you want to be respected. Adore no one. Love everyone.

~

The Third of the Twelve Commandments

3. You shall not take the name of the LORD your God in vain.
- Crusades have been fought, and natives slaughtered, in the name of a god that doesn't exist. How about that, in taking GOD's name in vain? Your deeds shall carry solely your name, not others'. For you are the only one responsible of your actions, and none other.

In the kingdom of LOVE, there is no wrong and no right.
In the space that has no beginning, and no end,
our name (ego/mind), we shall transcend.

~ Random ~

Jesus in the Temple

And Jesus entered the temple, with fury in his steps. There, He unleashed himself upon the people for their adultery with false gods. Gods of stone and gold. And looked with scorn at the jackal faced priests, who fill themselves with knowledge in order to feel superior over others.
"I shall burn down your false idols, whom you setup to fuel the illusion of separation. I tell you, that no building from whom you preach your own laws, shall withstand the rise of Love. For when It opens its eye, no thing of all that you think you are, shall remain.
For every man-made kingdom has its demise at the dawn of its creation. Yet, one shall stand, tall and proud, full of compassion towards all others and itself. This kingdom, shadows all others, not with grandeur, but with compassion and love, from which all is being nurtured to Life."

08.08.2016

~ Random ~

What is It about?

Only those that hold no fear, will come forth to me...
as the timeless children upon the gates of Heaven.

"I've sung my songs, and wept my weeps.
I've slept my nights, and dreamt my deeds.
I've bidden farewell to my lover, and kissed a friend.
I've treasured memories, and dug them a grave.
Each Dawn begets a new beginning."

It's time to move on from the emotional drama.

There will happen a time when we free ourselves from emotions. They are teachers as much as slavers. To feel (touch), we don't have to be emotionally involved. And no matter how convincing it might look, LOVE isn't found in emotions. They belong in the memories of past...let them stay there.

LOVE is here, greet it now!

Today looks like Sky is hanging low,
as if it longs for the fragrance of Earth.
For It has heard of my joy.

It listened while I greeted Love,
and as I kissed a friend, it sung.
"Hello again my love!"

02.10.2016 (...)

~ Random ~

San Pedro

Everything turned blades of shimmering black.
I heard myself becoming the distant echo,
of a rambling old man.

I became the sound that preceded the musical note.

I walk not in front of Him,
for I would only obscure his light.

Neither do I walk behind Him,
for the greatness of his shadow,
is the only deserving one.

There I walked, besides the Sun of Man...
He, who shoulders the mountains of this Earth.
The One, that becomes All.

~

Mankind will witness his rise within the darkness of Seed.
No eyes shall hold the sight of all this.
For in its greatness, Truth shall lay terror to their lies.

28.10.2016 (from beyond time)

~ Random ~

Let your tongue hold no words.
Let your lips be kissed...
As Silence speaks.

~ Random ~

French Alps *(journal extracts, fall of 2016)*

The following are extracts from my journal of when I visited a place called Aime-la-Plagne, in the French Alps. The initial reason I went there, was for a girl. Yet the purpose behind it, was far beyond my understanding. This is what followed.

~

As soon as the plane took air, I felt a deep vastness within my body, an opening of light between cells. Seeing the clouds get hit by the rays of the sun, roaming in blue seas of immense skies, I wanted to dive in this new-found love treasured within me. I experienced a certain readiness to die...but, I haven't yet seen it all.

~

I am just a body, who dances past by the death of this world.
So, shall I not sing tales about your eyes,
and of how they have conquered my mornings?

~

Before leaving, I embraced my Father. I wrapped my hands around him, as a mother does to her new-born son. It was there that I felt it. A lingering pain within him, inflicted by what was once me. Of that pain, I took some with me to the skies.

On my arrival, I shall seek the mountains and their snow, under which I shall bury this sourness of past. Alas it will bloom in the wildest of flowers, arising from the shadows to forever look towards the Sun.

May it be such.

~ Random ~

French Alps *(journal extracts, fall of 2016)*
cont...

Clouds hung so low, that you could see trees kissing them. Here, the obnoxious speed of man, hasn't yet arrived. While behind me all I could see, was the sky adorned in golden necklaces of clouds. My head spun with a restless pace, for dreams of young age, have been welcomed by the eyes of the man that yield them.

~

The landscape was getting brownish, trees resembling twigs, lakes more white and frozen still. I could hear nothing, except for the tiredness of the passengers' eyelids, being compensated by their lamenting voices. With the swoosh of air made by the sliding body of the train, I drifted off to a sleep.

~

Breathing in the chill air, coming from the depths of her eyes in tears, made my skin feel like the desert sand...thirsty and desiring more. The trees were upright towards the sky, and uprooted from the earth, as an offering dance to the silent Dame. Air made love to Water, giving birth to a crystallized whiteness that covered her breasts.

I desire to tell you more, yet Her land is mysterious, and open to understanding only to those who seek to be blinded.

~

~ Random ~

French Alps (journal extracts, fall of 2016)
cont...

Each morning I wake up, I see the mountains looking at me with their big white eyes. Even the clouds seem to be shy in getting close to them. I wonder what deeds they have witnessed and seen, and about the rumbling sound of their bellies. Sometimes they seem tickled by the movement of trees, that take residence on their cheeks.

~

Written words are how the time yet to come communicates with me. He talks in riddles. When it comes to writing, I can perceive a shift that brings the loss of time. The world around me crumbles down, and I am surrounded with a kaleidoscopic multiple choice.

That which my eyes gaze at, is committed to paper, and as such be destined to creation within this crystallized version of reality. Most times aware of my choosing, yet oblivious to which way and shape, destiny shall come to fruition.

~

Up at the stars, have my eyes gone,
that to which my heart has foretold.
Under a pine tree I rest my thoughts, savouring the warmth of soil,
as falling leaves melt the first of many skins of Snow.
So many winds have passed by,
yet the Earth kept her smell of dawning brown.
Thus, Her name has been transparently engraved,
with a fatherly touch upon the aliveness of it all.

"In patterns, if you may, please!
Far out in here, you will forget all grief."

~ Random ~

French Alps *(journal extracts, fall of 2016)*
cont…

She was all that they promised me She would be. A Virgin, of transparent skin, dancing in the shadows of the trees. I went closer to see, and closer...until the patterns that wrote poems of Her, revealed themselves everywhere I gazed. Here, underneath leaves, on a cushion of softest grass, we laid naked, singing to each other our intimate secrets.
And while I was leaving, She whispered her name, so that I will not forget her... "Forest"... She said.

~

If you ask my mother, she'll tell you. She'll recite childhood memories, which I don't have any recollection of. But mostly, she'll tell you how since always, I didn't talk much, and how I would question everything in front of me. What I remember from that vision of me is, how I would be in total awe with my surroundings. I would go into such detail, that all looked infinitely never ending. The smallest thing would be a grand monument raised from within the Earth by Nature herself, in the name of a GOD that can't be found because it's everywhere.

For that reason, I would shake or nod my head, or make sounds that have a yes or no meaning, instead of uttering out letters in conformed order. Words, since the day I could comprehend them, had a secondary, or even less, a value, compared to what I felt, experienced, and All else. Nothing could begin to describe what this Soul experienced through this body...both intertwined in the marriage of Life.

But now I see, in this coming of age, what power such words hold. For their origin resides within the translation from this Soul to its Body. Still, I don't like to talk much. If you come to me, I would prefer us to open fiercely our eyes, and just gaze spirallingly at each

~ Random ~

French Alps *(journal extracts, fall of 2016)*
cont...

other. For in you there are no words. There is only an endless, ravishing, Silence...on which our reflection gazes back at us. Shall you except this invitation, hold your tongue and just listen...it is here!

~

    My dreams are now but ripe fruit, whom I shall pick one by one. No seed shall be thrown away, as it is the beholder of more like her. I have envisioned faraway lands in my sleep, and it's their landscapes I pour out on paper. Yet, I have never smelled their fields, or climbed their hills, nor set under their trees. But there is a time of passing, and a time for deliverance. Hence in my creatorship there is now the longing of their fulfilment, where the time for them to bloom under the Sun, and weave under the stars...has come.

~

    Time...he ran through its roots, chasing after her, leaving trails of glistening gold. He didn't stop to listen, only to be known as wildly lost. She knew of his gaze, yet she never stopped to dance. She would halt in sheer gleam, and all the forest would fall on her in protection, for She was its pulsating heart.
    When Day and Night became a fading remembrance...birds and spiders came from all over do weave them a nest. By now His gaze became ghostly, His body weary...and Her silvery face has become pale, with eyes that stray. For the sake of Life beyond itself, one had to stop the chase, and the other the race. Both were being sought by Death, unless, they meet at this nest.
    So He ascended from the skies, knowing that He might not ever be again among the stars. From beneath the soil, and molten

~ Random ~

French Alps *(journal extracts, fall of 2016)*
cont...

rocks, She rose for her last time from under the belly of valleys and pillowed mountains.

With a vertical gaze at each other they stopped to listen, and for the first time truly witness. But this was the day that there had to be no wait. That was the reason why all had to stand hurriedly silent, even the tiger's claw stopped its killing, and trees their breathing. All stepped in to listen, at the moaning sound.

That was the time of no time, everything was conceivably one, as Father Sky made his entrance within Mother Earth. So bring forth your sorrows, and your tears, let them run wild and free, soaking the thirsty soil, thus bringing birth within the seed.

The flowering of their marriage was named Joy, meant to be the breath that guides all living things towards Love; the untimely!

~

As soon as I entered, I felt a warm embrace. An overwhelming feeling of warmth and peace, as if even the beat of my Heart stopped its race, to listen. My hands were as if they were constantly touching someone else's. Even the blackness of a seemingly burnt rock, was emanating Light, while the fire from the candles was whispering a sound, similar to that of underwater. My bones softened, my tissues halted from their contractions, my eyes became oceans reflecting the beauty of its Designer.

Physicians named it Energy. Religions call it God. It is what finds its creation within its own destruction. Hence it is eternal.

Never was a time, where It didn't exist.

~ Random ~

The reflection, can never judge its source.

~ Random ~

Notes

These longer texts came to me like ghosts during the days of January and February 2017. To be honest, I wasn't going to insert them in this book, since they have been posted on my Facebook profile. Yet, it was to that same exposure of social media, that you can find these texts here. I saw that, people found resonance with these texts. Being because, they challenge directly certain issues, without much glamour in the words. Here, they have been made available once again for sharing.

Among these words, there are my personal views, intimate thoughts and experiences, that have helped me to relief myself from the unnecessary suffering.

~

The "Need" to change the World

Few people know this, but I used to embrace the National Socialism beliefs, in short Nazism. Because that was my view of the world. In my eyes, the world and life within it, was harsh, and hard. Society taught us boys, that in order to become men, we have to show no feelings..."leave the emotional stuff to the girls!" And on my own, I found, that if I want to suppress my feelings, one way to do it is to direct all my energy and focus on fully hating someone. So, I directed all the hate and anger I could muster, according to the Nazi belief system. It was a systematic Self-killing mechanism. The fact that I was an introvert kept aiding this self-destructiveness. Who went through a period of introvert-ism knows fully well how the "need" to be understood overwhelms, and surpasses all else, hence it becomes relatively easy for hate and anger to take over. I was changing the world, by hating one person at a time. I didn't need to know you to hate you.

> Most of all, I hated myself for not finding the courage to express myself, all that I "really" felt.

Until three years ago, I couldn't understand the meaning of the words "conditioning", and "resentment". Through Rehabilitation I struggled with questions concerning such topics, always finding myself at a dead end. I wasn't able to access memories, because of emotional blockages. It was a year after Rehabilitation that the flood gates started to open, thanks to my first Ayahuasca ceremony. I re-lived all my past painful memories, and even up to the crucifixion of Jeshua. Who upon the cross, with his last breath, said; "Father, forgive them, for they don't know what they are doing." That vision, and the sound of those words, rippled throughout my whole body. The old walls of conditioning, and false belief systems, that have hidden me in the darkness of resentment and anger, were crumbling down. All of a sudden, I was floating among stars, and Light...Light...Light was I.

And of course, again, I wanted to change the world. A ridiculous task, that comes from the ego's avoidance, for not looking truthfully and honestly into oneself. Two years down the line...I realized that the world never changed. Since the first human attempt to record Life, till this day; war, greed, and lust for power over others, have been predominant throughout history. It is not in this modern age that we became sexually defiant. So, what changed?
I changed. The perspective from which I see things changed. I simply try and look within, so to gaze at the world with eyes of Love. That changed. And... surprise surprise...people around me started to change! My father, mother, brother...my boss, my colleague...they all changed! All I did was simply "no thing". I just started being less false, and more me.

~ Random ~

If you still feel the "need" to change the world...well...start by fully loving yourself. We all can do with some little more of self-love.

~

Most Times

Most days, I don't understand what am I doing. Most times, I am lost, wandering in a world beyond here. Most coffee breaks, I spend them talking with imaginary voices. Most of my actions are driven with arrogant behaviour. Most of my thoughts, regard the finding of a purpose. Most nights, I spend on the chase for a dream. Most of my days, I am running after a pair of lips in red. Most of my tears, are the falling of ink on paper.

In such moments as this one, which most people view as sad, or even dark, is the leaving of a chapter and the entry within another. It used to be a storm, and an emotional burden. Nowadays, it has become like the still reflective surface of a lake, upon which I am able to see all that I am not. Although it doesn't feel like it, because of the ego in grief, with its neediness towards emotions and attachments...for the Heart, and the Spirit that makes it beat...it is a time of great Joy and celebration, because another level of the lying mask is being shed.

Most people wish to be in the Light, and seen. Yet I ask, who is it that is being portraited out there for others to see? What part of us wishes to be seen? Most of my life I lingered in the shadow of others, cultivating anger for the lack of own expression.

Now, I am practicing in finding balance in all that. To be comfortable in my own shadow, and emanating my own light.

~ Random ~

"When your balls itch, and your mouth waters with lust...don't give in to all that. Instead, close your eyes, feel the softness of the Heart, and the Life in the Breath. Don't give in to the lie, but cultivate Truth...which is the "you" beyond all understanding and purpose." - that is what I am repeating to myself...every moment of everyday.

Most times, the hardest thing is to do nothing.

~

We Are Not Special

It is getting hard to distinguish between the dream state and the waking state. Dreams, as we conceive them, have nearly stopped. They come only when there is need for me to take action on something. Sometimes it is about a friend, other times it is about me experiencing "another" version of myself. For me there is no past life, but there is a space from where we all derive our existence, and it is from that space that visions of ancient memories are brought to us.

The deja vu's, and strong connections we feel with people that just came into our lives...not knowing how...they are all fragments of "what was", and still "is". Within Life, nothing goes wasted...we are a "recycled" body made out of particles that can never forever disappear. The same body that we find ourselves in, is the key. There is no purpose, and there is no meaning. It is our mind that tries to grab hold of such things, because without them it is lost, inexistent...dead...but we are not our mind.

With one seeking such things, one is distracted from the original design of nature. A flower doesn't ask why it has to bloom again in the morning, neither tries to be beautiful. Yet, it does, and is, all of that. Life takes care of itself, and we are Life...we just forgot that we are eternal and infinite...space!

I don't seek a god to pray to, or a master to follow. I just wake up before the Sun, to hear its voice and guidance, my listening. Or I approach a tree, for strength and connectivity with Earth. And there are the Waves, which are my favourite. They love telling stories about their relationship with the rocks and sands of the Shore, and how they came to shape the land.

All is perceived by us, with the same way that we "see" ourselves...that is our dictionary, which varies from one person to the other. There is no same meaning for the same word, because our lives have been all unique. We are not "special". We simply have been shaped differently, according to our choices...and everyone is...like that.

There are no words, for the same "language" that was meant to bring us together, has brought us apart. In silence, we can all come to know each other much better.

~

What is this Urgency?

People claiming to have arrived to a certain stage in their lives, start to feel the urge in "pushing" others to change.

I have felt that urge too, and it was only after, that i realized it was only my arrogance, coming from the false belief that I have achieved something, and that others have to acknowledge and follow. It was that same false belief that anchored me to a "fixed" point. Thanks to that, I was resisting the change within me.

~ Random ~

Who am I to say that the world needs changing, or fixing?

Who am I to urge others to wake up to their awakened state?

Why? Am I, myself fully awake?

Why? Am I, not loving the contrast that all "without" provides, and which I myself created?

And wasn't that same contrast that provided the light to shine upon my path?

The want to change or fix the world, is a form of escape from that something in us we haven't yet excepted.

We don't need healing in any form, except for the one that helps us to shed the false beliefs of "who we are".

We can only be what we are...in that purest form, there is perfection. The rest, is again the imposition of others, upon others.

I don't seek a teacher, a master, a guru, or a god. I seek the Love I am made of. In this seeking, there is the desire of relating to the One that is All.

Stop...and listen...

~

Do I really have to be happy?

You know when, people ask; "how are you?"

~ Random ~

This question used to put me in a dilemma. Like; "what should I answer, when I don't even know myself?" Forcing myself to go into, an on the spot inquiry of my feelings and emotions.

In the past, I felt a "need to feel", otherwise it was like I wasn't even living. I had to "have" things, and my "wants" fulfilled, so that I would be happy. But to satisfy those "wants" and "needs", the road was paved with pain. Happiness had a great cost. A price that was never paid in full, because what I was buying never came to be mine.

Emotions are a great driving force, which take people to seek different things, among them is relationships. We seek, in order fill that emptiness inside...and that emptiness is GOD!

On the road of seeking, we get drunk by emotions, coming from disappointments, lack, and loss. They become like a drug, a dependency. Something that we "need" to "feel" alive.

Where do I go, to seek what I already have?

See emotions rise, as the morning sun and the stars of night. Let them fill your whole being with joy and peace, knowing that they are not you, but signs to show you the way. A sign doesn't move, don't become that. Read your own Life book, knowing that you are not the protagonist, but the author.

I personally have lately been experiencing less and less drunken escapades with emotions, because I know that I am alive. There is nothing that can make me "more", or "less", alive. Life is not about "this" and "that". Life is.

I am "not" what I am seeing or feeling. But am I the one perceiving all of that.

~ Random ~

For a better mis-understanding

Our trying to understand, or figure out each other, brings us to "miss" the whole point, or the actual thing that we wish to come and know.

We are bound to interaction, with things, persons, and surroundings. How we perceive, and interpret all that, is up to us. The knowledge, and experiences, gained from our past, help us to formulate a dictionary, which gives "meaning" to what is happening now. That "meaning" is prone to judgement and assumptions, hence it is false. It builds an idea of ourselves which is not true, nor real.

This false idea of ourselves, creates a fictitious personality which we believe it is us. A personality full of "needs", requiring constant attention and acknowledgement, because otherwise it faces death. This personality takes different roles; parent, teacher, son, daughter, addict, etc... depending on the circumstances than at hand.

This personality is the reason why we suffer.

It suffers because, it tries to live up to the expectations of others upon it, and of itself. These expectations are never met. Like a dog chasing its tail, it is caught in a loop. Thinking it is going somewhere, when in reality it is lost in its own identification of trying to do something.

The past is called like that, because it has "passed". We are "now and here" in a totally different space.

How long will we keep on trying to resurrect, what is already dead?

~ Random ~

Don't we want to live in harmony with our present, ourselves and others?

For how long we will keep labelling ourselves with situations that we have already overcome?

    We all have been given a name, a religion, a status in society, etc... Yet it is not those things and labels, that make our body move. They are just costumes and masks, to try and cover-up the truth, which is the awareness of oneself.

~

Laugh at your own insecurities. See how that makes you feel, and tell me about it.

Take nothing "personal", and see how it feels.

Forget who you are.

Let go of everything that you think you know.

Leave nothing.

See what remains. Come, and speak about it.

~

    We have called upon Love, many a thousand times. Yet we have shivered away from it, because, Love is not personal. In fact, it transcends all that.

Are we ready to truly, and honestly, meet Love?

~

~ Random ~

Don't seek Spirituality. Be Humanity.

What is it that has to be?

Since my book has been publicized, people have shown their support in various ways. I guess we all have that one person within our family, that has struggled, or still is, with drug addiction. The other version could be that, that person is in fact me.

Beyond addiction, there is something that everyone can relate to, in one way or the other. That "something" is pain! Drugs, and other things that are self-destructive, are just tools that we use to "try" and mask/numb that pain. Great is the wish to break free from it, yet we identify, and twistedly crave it too much, to see ourselves pain free. What you see in my words, is the breakthrough from that pain. I can recall my past, and describe it to you, many times over, and yet I won't bring up the suffering of those days.

I am now "mostly" pain free, because I have forgiven that which didn't need forgiveness.

Can you see yourself beyond pain?

Can you see that you have a choice? - Every moment of every day, you are a choice!

Pain makes you think you are special, even gifted. Because you're "feeling", "seeing" so much! Dwelling in the rough seas of emotions, never to set sail towards the freedom of Dawn.

Make, that choice.

Within the last months, my process was focused mainly on to shed all those layers that hold me back from being what I truly

~ Random ~

am. I see it as the constant flowering of Life, which now isn't driven by inquiry. All that has been slowly left behind, to give space to Self-Presence. My body is left doing its thing, with the required speed. Yet my inner world, rests for most of its time, untouched, uninfluenced, within a realm of peace, of soft and slow untimely going. Believe me when I tell you, "it has become effortless".

Yet, there is no success or achievement in all of this. All I did was to drop that set of "thousand keys", which was dragging me down and burdening my pockets since young age. "Keys" that asked me to find them a lock.

There is none. The Heart has always been open.
I just didn't see that.

Yet, with this...I haven't gone to a further stage, or development. On the contrary. I just went "inside"...where I am human before anything else...within a home that still hosts all sorts of cravings, and desires. Yet, instead of indulging in one another, we sit quietly and observe each other...because...we are one of the same.

Don't seek spirituality. Be Humanity.

~

~ Random ~

Wrap You up in Dreams

I don't wish to know you name.
I want to know your dreams, and how you fly into them.
I want to know how you take your coffee, and how you wrap your hands around its cup.
I want to know what you have lost, and the pain it caused.

I want to ride the shine of your hair, just to glide it around your ears.
I want to see you wake up, and how the Sun is shadowed by your beauty.
I want to drown in the skies, that make up the colour of your eyes.
I want to hear the golden sand, that clings with thirst to your skin.

To know if you're sad in your loneliness...
...just to let the voice of raindrops washing it away.

To know what the stars and their signs have to say...
...just to let them fall gently as tears in their glory.

To know what your heart longs for...
...just to meet it there in all the silence that is Love.

29.01.22017 (from a stranger and a lover)

~ Random ~

Among the Sands

Among the sands that embrace your feet, lies the story of my Love,
carved with memories that ride my Soul like Summer waves.

Have you any more of that rain in your pockets?
Those drops that laid beds of rainbows for our play.

Thoughts of you fill my home,
with your voice suspended in the midst of the air I breathe.
It is the past whom I cleared out, that left an emptiness,
becoming a bed for you to rest your heart.

Dreams stopped in their coming,
for they became all that I see within you.

Under the warm darkness, of the blanketed night sky,
your curious eyes perch upon my sleep…just to read the signs
written by the stars.

For it was a wise man with golden hair, that foretold this coming.
With strings of violin, he told me about you,
and of the glimmer that adorns your face.

Words of comfort, that brought peaceful tears,
were the seeds that bloomed in a flower of water and fire.

30.01.2017 (from a stranger and a lover)

~ Random ~

Her Coming

She is waiting there,
among the smouldering ashes of a dying fire...
ready to set it up again ablaze!

Her, is the Fire that beds the Ocean,
the Forest that takes root upon the mountain,
the Thunder that dances through Heaven.

Only the golden Clouds foretold Her coming,
With voices of Snow in Summer.

I found comfort in my own death,
As a peaceful emptiness, it left.
For Her, it will be a throne,
From where Love overflows...

01.02.2017 (from a stranger and a lover)

~ Random ~

Pen

Tell me, my beloved Pen…
I am here to listen to your desire,
of how you want me to move you.
Show me how you want my hands,
to be wrapped around your neck.
I plead you to guide me breathless,
through lines of favourite positions and pleasure.
If it hurts please scream,
so, I can feel your pain and hear your moan.

Although Silence puts us apart,
rest assured that I am not far.
For I shall always keep you in my pocket,
to always carry you, and your body with me.

To write the next word,
and fill the last endless page.

January 2017

~ Random ~

Where Wild Daffodils Grow

I sought this place of silence, for many a year,
free from all corruption and pain.

And it came to be, that I moved in you…
Daughter, born out of water,
Child, of the Moon and its Tide.
Washed ashore by the surfing waves,
with gleaming eyes like pearly shells.

And like the trees that seek the skies,
In her desire is the dance of earthly fire.

In all of this I met you…
An Angel bathing in stars,
Gently disturbing my sleep.

I am now robbed from all words by your lips,
Staring silently at the kiss beneath your feet,
Watching the birth of wild daffodils.

February 2017

~ Random ~

Unfold

There she is, naked and bathing in stars.
Surrounded by angels, waiting for their turn to dance.
Taking her time, in counting the lights of night, one by one.

Bold enough to seek, but cowardly scared,
I have locked away a part of me, afraid that she will steal it.
On my knees, I am pleading Change to make its part.

She comes fearlessly close, with eyes of flowering thunder.
Taking into her hands my body, so to step into her.
Walls of old come crumbling down, within her arms.

And She smiles... in the showing of Love.
With hair of golden streaks, and lips of dawn,
Changing the colour of darkness with a moan.

The voice of her pale pearly skin,
Brings to life what was distant and dying.

"Let me lift you up,
while the wings of angels,
unfold for us this bed."

February 2017

~ Random ~

Here

My mind wants relentlessly to speak to you.
Yet my heart has nothing to say...it is simply silent.

For even the most beautiful of languages,
is foul in its description of Love.

So here I am, laying peacefully in the eye of the storm.
...here, I am with you, and Love.

24.01.2017 (from a stranger and a lover)

~ Random ~

Love is you

~ Random ~

The Lost Poems

The following poems where lost among the endless writings that I put down. They were hidden in pages of old journals, and in my mismanagement of the writing application. *The Shorts*, are a rapid fire of sudden realisations, and shifts in space. *The Later*, are a series of poems written savagely on paper, in the months of Summer 2017. Therefore, some will carry a name, while others won't.

~

Oh my Queen

Oh my Queen, who took your crown?
Was that King, that behaved like a clown?
Or that selfish Lover,
Bound only to desire?
A sacrificial lamb on a throne,
Where your heart became of stone.
No longer you weep,
No longer you sleep.
In your icy eyes of Life no flame,
I want to know for such sin who is to blame!
Let the bell toll for this perpetrator,
And him be judged by the Creator.
When done is the deed,
On my knees I will plead,
For my soul your heart to reach, to kiss.
Together we'll live in Utopian bliss!

01.10.2014 (written against women oppression and abuse)

~ Random ~

My Payment

They taught me that I should feel guilty,
For I was born with sin.
But whose sin?
That of lovers wanting to be in each other,
succumbing by nature to their desire?
That of two lovers that just wanted to be gods?
Why? Aren't we all gods?
All creators of our own reality?
Aren't we the chosen and the choosers?

They programmed me as such,
I knew only as much.
I was bound to mistake and sin.
Imprisoned in the desolation of mind fields.
I paid for the illusion with poison in blood,
with time and constant suffering,
with demons up and down my spine,
with putrid waters out of my skin,
with shattering teeth,
with screams of earthquaked bones.
I paid for their fear,
For the anger of letting them do this to me.

I paid...
For that reality which was a fantasy,
For that fantasy to be my reality.

For the right to wake up, and dream.

17.01.2015 (written after a fierce wake up)

~ Random ~

Metamorphosis

My stomach turns in a painful bind,
Coming from a call to leave all behind.
An urge to crawl and kiss the land.
Fingers as claws bury themselves in sand.
I growl at the pale moon in screaming pain,
Looking at the water I can't remember my name.
A pair of wings in blood soaked feather,
To your echoing voice I surrender.
In this stranger's eyes a thirst,
Who will he carry first?

30.06.2016 (written in Comino during a night of...)

~

Spanish Girl

At night in search, She roams the streets,
For a dreamer to wipe off his feet.
Her eyes pierced with the Moon's light,
Tender lips in kiss hold each other tight.
Bronze skin tricked the Devil into falling in love,
In his heart, the seed of desire had sprout.
Her golden hair shining as the silent desert,
Sighing stories of men from whom she got hurt.
From the plains and beaches of Spain,
The wind echoes the beauty of her name.
A softness in her body shakes off the Sun,
With open arms She welcomes what's to come...

.l.o.s.t. (from a stranger)

~ Random ~

Wedding Dress of Black

She rose from the soils of the forest...
hair dark as the Night in its black wedding dress,
wild eyes in the turquoise blue of the Day's naked sky,
skin meticulously knitted in lace of fireflies,
and with a voice violent as Birth and sweet as Death.

Her inhaling breath took in all the sorrow of man,
while her exhale filled all with a vibrating joy.

She looked upon the trees,
in dance with the warm southern winds,
as the northern mountains roared with thunder.
She paused...
and smiled the whitest of lights...
an eternal blinding love.

.l.o.s.t.

~

Her beauty is inevitable.
So much so that her skin is laced with glowing snow.
The air around her smells of roses and innocent grandiosity.
She finds in my memory her immortality,
throughout my roots lies her truth.
Together we followed the footsteps to the edge of time,
Where the stars sang old songs with words in rhyme.
There we laid...floating in space...
As the Sun kissed her face...
I adorned Her with freedom,
To roam my lonely kingdom.

.l.o.s.t.

~ Random ~

The Shorts

She gently stripped away her nakedness,
and veiled herself in night.
Such is, that man came to dream.
No one saw her coming down the road of the spit snake,
dragging along the illusion of religion.
She had already decided...it's time to kill,
so the blind will come to see.

~

And She bleeds Love with her rays in red.
Oh lady from space, come and kiss this face.
Succumb to the desire, of A Heart in fire.

~

They say that a man should never lay hands upon a woman.

I say lay them!
Lay them, as long they have the dirt of a day's work.
Lay them stained with the blood of longing.
Lay them,
as you would lay your weary head on the pillow at night.
Lay them,
as the sailor would hold the ropes of Sails though storms.
Lay them...as you would try to grab water...
for the next moment holds her disappearance in the morning mist...
with her body subtle as kiss.

~

~ Random ~

The Morning held a knife, with which he took my wife.
Day turned black, and I vouched to take Her back.
So as soon as evening was violated by Moon,
begun my duty of groom.

I went to Soil with a shuffle, my voice in muffle,
to lay a bed upon Her death.
It was there where roses bloomed their many faces of Grace.
In each other we found our Selves, and the purpose to serve.

~

There is a ferocity to her soft touch,
and tenderness in her violent eyes.

~

The quest, of the question,
is to find its mark.

~

The Universe will never hold us back from the things we love.
Only our own fear does.

~

Don't greet me outside of yourself.
But let me meet you,
in the longing of your own Heart.

~

~ Random ~

The Later

Although I wish for your nakedness,
It is the same dream that dies,
When I stare into your eyes.

So as my lips touch in between your legs,
There comes, the infinity of stars in space.

~

After searching the treacherous seas,
I have found you sleeping on a gentle wave.
It was your bare chest that caught my gaze.

Shall you now, let me take you home?

~

Strands of golden hair in between my fingers.
Hands clutch at sheets, as sweat dries in rivers.
Every exhale, a thump of the water that falls.
Lips biting each other in breathless moans,
Neck stiffens at the pleasure of pain,
Appeased by a shivering game.
Tongues search for a new thrill,
The yet unkissed and salty skin;
Just enough for the buds to come alive.
The inhale, and endless grit…
Existence in a drift.
An ageless craving,
As a violin in orgasm.

~

~ Random ~

Come…
Come…whoever you are!
See me search the mirror for that shadow.
Come…
And tell me about the legends,
that ruled upon the Heart of Moon…
of Her lands in flowering bloom.

~

At first sight, you see only a glimpse; a flash of light, that fastens its way to disappear. It comes in the softest of breezes, stars that approach shyly the Night. A dance of dusk, in traces without rush, paves the way through your lips. Lay…look at the ceiling of sea in blue…

Waves of Moon's bright white,
beyond which your eyes go and hide.
Sheets filled with tender sighs,
Beneath which your legs tease.
…of lust and its fiery wings.

Let me be silent for the hushing sound,
Of your body against mine,
For it is to what they will leap tonight.

19.08.2017 (the girl in ink)

~

A heart weaved from angels broken wings.
Threads spun out of stars and time,
Searching obsessively the end of eternity.
She knew the first flight of this Earth and its Moon.
Old, but young as this very Heart.
…of fingers and webs…of birth and its maze.

~ Random ~

*Would you leave it
Up to Destiny;
If you knew
You could change it?*

~ Random ~

Intimacy Exposed

Darkness, is a mere definition of what our mind cannot conceive. It simply captures the duality within which we "choose" to exist.

These text were written out of the immediate experience within interaction, and mostly in morning wakeups. It is in that time of day, that I am mostly inspired, when the Sun comes out from just outside my bedroom window. A black coffee enthusiast. An explorer of solitude. A lover of leaving.

~

5th September 2017 morning

No one taught me your language, how to dance to your voice, or what to do when you become silent and beautifully ravishing. I had to discover all that on my own, by daring to come and breathe in your skin, to stand here amidst the breeze of your unmoving lips.
"Come in me my love...let your eyes pave the way with a carpet of tears. You knew me out of the longing of your heart. Now you will drink, and live in me, upon Life's unwavering sheets" - She said.

5th September 2017 evening

This is how it is for me; I wake up - I write, I eat - I write, I have coffee - I write, I sleep - I write, I walk - I write. I might not write on paper or some other device - but I write. Who writes knows, how the words become one, like blood with veins.
The following is what I wrote while I was walking towards my daily swim;

"Don't wake the sea", they said.

At the first sight, of her blossoming in blue, I could not help but crave...of touch and its slide...of mouth and its hinging tongue.

~ Random ~

She stood there, among the waves of water and clouds, like an angel in its birth of flight.

How can I, not awake this Sea of arousing sighs?

6th September 2017 evening

Even if I wanted to, I can't bring myself to explain what the last 20 days were about.

It's just that there are so many things that we dismiss, and it's not that it is necessary to talk and share about them. In fact, I saw that it was more beneficial not to talk sporadically about them. I just had to accept them as part of my space, which takes a certain level of self-awareness. It took me the whole 20 days to find my peace again amidst the storm of emotions. In such times, poetry takes a different shape as well, it is like this mistress in dark royal hair, to which I succumb in thoughts and heart. She takes me to roam, like black wolves that stare out from the shadows, where Pen becomes Claw, and Paper shapes into Skin.

Thunder praised fear, clouds rang of lust, and stars smelled of sex, while my fingers felt like claws desiring flesh.

An unruly world, is the one that lives in me...for what is an Artist, if not someone that challenges the known boundaries of reality?

12th September 2017 evening

Staring blindly at every corner, burdened with undesirable feelings; like ravens squawking...I kept telling myself; "this is just another normal day, nothing to over analyse. It will pass, for nothing lasts. Breathe, and try to be gentle with yourself. Soon Night will come, and sleep will take this away."

That's how it was yesterday for me; I was lost in loss, not knowing where, how, or why. Couldn't concentrate, nor I could hold things safely in hand. As the ritual goes, I arrived home, made my black Mocha&Santos coffee, and sat down on my desk. Trying to find the thread, that would save me from this confusion; my mobile screen lit by a message I was waiting for 24hours. It was her, from the other side of the world. She accepted, and the thread was seen weaving a creation of such a misunderstood expression; "Sexuality". Within a few exchanged words, a mutual friendship with an unusual surprising depth developed; seemed that we saw the same story in each other's photographic eyes.

13th September 2017 morning

I want the ice, and its shivering cold, who simply ignores my breath. I want its gripping edge, that cuts through my lips in search for kiss. I want it to build a bed of snow, upon which skin rises in shivers. I want it to show up like curtains of mist, behind which our bodies will meet, oblivious to the freeze...naked and lost...not knowing who's who...where's what...am I you?

I am the circling undying Fire in pyres. She is the Queen of frozen air and water, who's strong cheeks and chin, in my dreams I've always seen.

19th September 2017 morning

So I go to make my morning black and murky coffee, and I am reminded of how much I am in love with Shadows; the comfort of solitude they offer, the place from where I can see and not be seen. Everything loses its definition, and all fades into this bed of man in flesh. I don't know who am I, so many actors and play-writers in me, who like to supersede each other. They are quite a bunch, and I stand here, amused by this drama they so hard try put up. So from the dark gallery of the theatre; I watch this love for Life, that has given birth to this body, whom just wishes to explore more of the skin, and its sweaty nakedness.

"They" dressed me in labels, and stung me with achievements. Yet I have burnt them with the same passion and transgression, that my pen penetrates the paper.

Have you known man, and woman?

~ Random ~

Where you not taught one or the other?
What is sex anyway?
Have you even given flight to Utopian idealism?

He can't live without Her, and She cannot breathe without him.
Yet, in here, both are birthed within one another.

20th September 2017 morning

To live in insecurity is not for everyone. We cling and hang on to "who we think we are", as if our existence depends on it. Yet what we think of ourselves, is a mere projection of our desires.

We try to be and achieve,
in order to give a purpose to our doing and living.
We give too much so to be loved.
We mask ourselves in order to be seen.

Yet Life asks nothing of us. It created us from emptiness itself. So if we truly want to be free, we have to undress from the ideas we have of ourselves. Only when naked, we will be like the wind that greets the waves, the sun that burns in its longing to touch the earth, and as I, seeking to kiss your chest.

Have you ever made love to yourself?

28th September 2017 morning

I am sure, that our dreams to which we aspire to, always come true, the moment we let go of the "idea" of how they should be fulfilled. The path is rich with opportunities, which we can't see, unless we remove our own ideals of ourselves, life, and love. The same ideals, that restrict us from being all that which we aspire to. The ideals that keep us hanging on to what we know.

~ Random ~

What we wish and aspire to, lies in a path unknown to us. In that unknown, our dreams are like ripe fruits, ready to be savoured.

Come, be empty of you (past),
so that your desires can be true.

1st October 2017 morning

I love the world as it is, with all its likes and dislikes. With all its people, smells, landscapes, and destruction. The spices, the ashes, the long paths through forests, and men on horseback. I especially love women; the scent left on the pillow, their skin after a swim in the sea, the sweetness and yet ferocity upon their wake up, their relentless drive towards love and its making, that no man can ever match to. "More!!!" is what comes out of their lips.

I love the Sun, with its nourishing warm, and the way it unveils the Night, the time when the Moon slowly slowly goes in hide. I love the world; as it is - and I am not planning to go try and change it any time soon.

With a kiss she killed my prayers

As penetrating as the breath that goes into the lungs, so is that we held each other, moaning for more, out of attachment to this life and its pleasures. You wake up from the dream, full of desires and frenzy, with a body that supplicates for the other to surrender.

1st October 2017 evening

Don't seek me among the veils of faces,
which hide the truth among a cowardly crowd.
I am the nomad, that wanders amidst the spectrum of light.
Only there, I am myself...for I have no colour.
I am the space in between the face, and its mask.

~ Random ~

2th October 2017

It is always hard to describe, when it comes to this. It is not about the beauty perceived, but about the "one" who creates it. The definition of such a word, doesn't exist, for it works in dynamic with one's current "state of being". It is there, that I am a perfectionist. In the realm of "beauty", I am lost between the curves of clouds, and woman's hips (yes, woman is singular). Lost amidst the texture of the sky, and the colour of Her holographic eyes / the golden rays of the Sun, and the endless stream of particles making up Her skin / the rough edges of mountains, and the shardy corners of Her lips.

She/Her; is an idea, a projection created from within my dreams. Yet I feel She exists, for I have seen Her in Love between blinks.

Come my beloved, I am waiting patiently at my home's edge
...bed is ready, and coffee is warming up sparingly.

4th October 2017 morning

The Wind kept blowing strongly, all through Night, and Thunder
lightened up pieces of the Sky.

Didn't sleep well. While in bed, it felt like a waking dream, in between leaving and staying. Faces visited me, and very vividly; I don't like that, it feels like they want too much from me. ~
At least in the morning, there's the blackness of Coffee to stare into; boiling hot, She arises from the steam of the Mocha pot.

Doesn't say a word, but just points with her glance,
for me to look, inside.
There was her body, full of grace;
like the Night, She was naked in between the Earth and Stars.

~ Random ~

7th October 2017

How selfish is, he that wants to change the world?

I see nothing wrong with the world. It's colourful, mysterious, and yet open to discovery. The Hindi have a goddess; her name is Kali. She is the destructive force within Life and Nature. In her dance, there is the end, and death of illusion. By illusion, we mean the "ideas" we have if ourselves; that which we "think" we are, and since it's just a thought, it is not real.

I had, and still have, prefixed "ideas" of myself, which lately I have come to see how much they have hindered my relation to others, and myself. They keep me from growing and connect. I have come to realize that; although I "see" myself in a certain way, that which is "seen", is not me, but a mere projection of my mind. In truth, I am the "seer". Great power lies beyond that realization. Great freedom and joy has been found, deep beneath those layers of "ideas".

I can now express myself in so many different ways, without feeling ashamed, or judged, for it is coming out from the heart. The portrayal of ourselves, is our self-expression. So go, and simply express what you feel, become your dream, even if it is for a moment, and let it be captured in the eternity of memory; knowing that you are the actor, and not the role.

8th October 2017

Today, I woke up with a so familiar feeling of nostalgia, amidst the
sheets of an empty bed. I have been in pursue of what you call
Love, for most of the given Life. My eyes see Her upon their own
reflection. It is like a veil between my sight, and that which is seen.
I know it is there, within me. Yet the reason why I can't reach it, is
because I go for it with my hands.

~ Random ~

So I went to pen and paper, and got me more confused. After many tries, I decided to bridge this illusionary distance with tears, falling slowly within the space between heart beats.

"My eyes are in tears,
Just for them to hit,
Like graceful waves your feet.
A mouth in shores,
Wet by its own words in want of more.
She is painted upon a body,
By Love and its folly."

End of October 2017

The Moon, that shone so brightly through last night, while I was paving through dreams, and an obscure destiny, is now become a memory, fading within the red and violet-blue of the morning sky. Sitting here alone, for it is here that I find you; always singing while you desire to undress me. You are quick, and yet gentle, in taking off that lavender gown, which takes its time in surrendering to gravity. With your pale face that keeps showing, like pine cones affixed to the bony branches to a never aging tree, and a stare that spirals out so to reach the essence of all that I am; I feel like the Woman that has the Man inside her - penetrated like the breath that fills a hollow reed. Within myself, I seek for you, an angel that fell the damned stairs of Heaven, as every time I call you in prayer, all naked and sacred, under these bedsheets you appear.

How shall I explain, to those that read, that the place to look for, is the in between; whom surrounds every word, and every line, veiling Life in a mystery of hide and seek.

~

~ Random ~

Akasha

And so it happened that I found myself in love, not having the sweet remembrance of its becoming. Not even the slow rise of Sun from the East, could have heaped in so silently. It has no voice, for She is what sound travels upon;

> of skin in bronze brown,
> of the first sky and cloud gowns.

That moment where our chests touched in an embrace, I could feel the earliest of fires whom kindles her ravishing pulse, a face adorned with fierce white eyes like ice, untouched from the heat of her own heart. The dark starry night is reflected within her hair, let to fall down upon shoulders like thousand-year-old smouldering ashes, sustained to breath with streaks of flaming red.

> Saw her dancing all the while,
> upon waves of air and the Moon's glare.
> We shared time, space, and two distant beds;
> as two souls upon the flowering of innocence.

25.09.2017 (a sudden encounter...of Love and the Surface of Sound)

~ Random ~

Her favourite colour is Black

She sees her own daylight within the same dreams of night. That is what makes her whole, encompassing the eternal dusk-dawn, ruling the pathways that give birth to the fluorescent light. In her wonder, thunder flashes through lenses, for the sake of fulfilling her desires;

of Life and its belonging,
of attraction in its law-making.

Her thoughts are waves, whom like stars, adorn the emptiness of space. As perfume they linger in the thin air, giving Future a faithful face. Shrouded in mystery, her eyes perch out from behind a veil of darkened hair, as to their destiny they stare. Upon her head, a lavender crown, slightly wearing a translucent gown. She strides proudly forward, ignoring all judgment and howls.

She made herself to be a Queen of Dreams,
whose reign are the cat-walking streets.

Let Man stare.
Let his understanding fail.
Let him lust after his own game.

Let Her be,
what She already is…
Life!

19.10.2017 (to the girl that made the cover of this book possible)

~ Random ~

Revealing the Truth

Change implies many things, and at the same time, none at all.

We take on different masks and forms, depending on different situations and environmental influences. So how can we come to know what mask we are wearing, since most times we ourselves, are not even aware of the mask itself?

Many of us venture out in the world to discover more of who they really are. I chose to venture inside; whether it is the mind or the heart space, it is all happening within and without me. Each and every one of us has a personal structure, which most call ego. I prefer to call it "persona", since the word ego for most people has an inherited understanding of something negative. The "persona" is part of our survival mechanism, it helps us to project ourselves in a certain way so to enjoy interaction with others.

Don't judge it.

It is like when we wear clothes. The clothes we wear, are in accordance to the places and occasions that we are going for. And it is pretty simple to understand, because now that I have told you this, you can become aware of how you feel "changed" from wearing your pyjamas, to wearing a suit. We are all actors on stage, playing a role within this multi-diverse play called Life. It is always beneficial to know "who is" the actor, and what role has he/she found him/herself acting. I have always wished to get and know that, because acting without knowing exactly what, made me uncomfortable and anxious when I had to be around people.

Each and every one of us, has his/her own vibration, and it's basically unique to every individual. Coming to sense, and be in that vibration, leads one to genuinity; the highest creative unconditioned force there is.

A human being.

I always knew how to relate to the space between me, and what was perceived. Yet I didn't know how to relate to people. They seemed strange, out of a "false inherited" behaviour and hype that I could never understand and resonate with. My interests where further away from what most get engulfed in. In a way, no particular thing, has ever caught my full interest. One of the reasons, can be that I am in nature a fast learner, I absorb things rapidly. Maybe that's why I than get bored easily. Nothing has ever got my attention so fervently as the quest to know who I am. That was always my only invested interest, which felt like an obligation I had towards myself, and a responsibility towards others. But it's out of that quest that I started disassociating myself from most. I dismissed completely the lifestyle most people lived, ending up dismissing completely the people who I deemed not fit of any interest and curiosity. I made up a story, around a character defined as an introvert and shy. That is the persona I chose to be.

The real visible change, happened when I decided that I don't want to be that any more. Deep within me I always craved interaction and relation, and this persona, was hindering all that, and of course my growth. Today I try in the best way I can, to be aware of these barriers, caused out of judgment for self, so that I can enjoy myself and others within a space of spontaneity;

Being!

Seeing and looking at our own illusions,
is much more fun than being them.

What I *think* I am, cannot be more further away from Truth.

~ Random ~

It is time to go,
Beyond…

www.ingramcontent.com/pod-product-compliance
Lightning Source LLC
Chambersburg PA
CBHW051649040426
42446CB00009B/1058